REDEEMING RELEVANCE

IN THE BOOK OF EXODUS

EXPLORATIONS IN TEXT AND MEANING

REDEEMING RELEVANCE

IN THE BOOK OF EXODUS

EXPLORATIONS IN TEXT AND MEANING

RABBI FRANCIS NATAF

URIM PUBLICATIONS
JERUSALEM · NEW YORK

DAVID CARDOZO ACADEMY

Redeeming Relevance in the Book of Exodus:
Explorations in Text and Meaning
by Rabbi Francis Nataf

Copyright © 2010 by Francis Nataf

Printed in Israel
First Edition

ISBN 978-965-5240-37-5

Urim Publications, P.O. Box 52287, Jerusalem 91521 Israel
Typeset by Ariel Walden

Lambda Publishers Inc.
3709 13th Avenue Brooklyn, New York 11218 U.S.A.
Tel: 718-972-5449 Fax: 718-972-6307, mh@ejudaica.com

www.UrimPublications.com

In memory of HENRY FREIER, *z"l*,
a child survivor of the Holocaust from Slovakia,
who despite all of the suffering,
continued to have a strong love for Judaism
and the Jewish people.
May we follow the path he laid out for us.

DAVID and ILENE BROOKLER

In Memory of my father,
RICHARD BLOOM
(Chayim Reuven ben Yisrael)

ANDY BLOOM

CONTENTS

ACKNOWLEDGEMENTS

As with my first book, there were many people involved in the creation of the present volume. Beyond the people I will mention are all the teachers, colleagues, students, friends and relatives who have made an impact on my perceptions of, and approach to, the Torah. I have taken all their input and made it into my own unique synthesis of the text, but that does not prevent it from also being theirs.

My association with the David Cardozo Academy in Jerusalem for the last seven years has been a labor of love. It has given me the opportunity to interact with many outstanding and creative individuals who have collectively provided a nurturing spiritual and intellectual community. To its Dean, Rabbi Dr. Nathan Lopes Cardozo, I am eternally grateful for his concern, support and encouragement. I wish him and his family much success in all their endeavors. Our administrative assistant, Mrs. Esther Peterman, has diligently used her formidable talents to help in this project as she does with whatever tasks are presented to her. For this I thank her very much.

The Academy's friends and supporters have provided me with the aid and interested feedback that is so critical to any writing project. In particular, I want to thank my friends Andy Bloom, David and Ilene Brookler, Morris Dweck and David Sassoon for their support in this endeavor. Their constant involvement in worthwhile projects serves as a source of personal inspiration and makes me thankful to be associated with them. May they always inspire others with their good work.

I want to express my appreciation to Tzvi Mauer and all the fine people at Urim Publications for their help and support over the years. As a writer, it is important to have a publishing house that feels like one's home. For me, Urim is certainly that and more. In particular, I would like to thank Ariel Walden and Sara Rosenbaum. To the various teachers and colleagues, Rabbi Dr. Nathan Lopes Carodzo, Rabbi Yitzchok Adlerstein, Rabbi Dr. Joshua Berman, Rabbi Shalom Carmy, and Rabbi Nathaniel Helfgot, who all looked over the manuscript, I will always be grateful.

Last but not least, I would like to thank my family. My wife, Deena, put her finest efforts into editing this book. Before her revisions, it was far from ready for publication. Putting it into its current form was nothing short of a *tour de force*. I thank her for her encouragement in this project and in everything worthwhile that I do. I also want to thank my children, Yoel, Amalia, Tamar and Saadia, for their interest and support. The same is true of my mother, Mireille Nataf, and my in-laws, Sheldon and Marion Cohen.

A friend of mine who just finished writing his first book told me that one book in a lifetime is enough for him. At one point in my life, even that was just a dream. But to have my second book published and available to the general public is the realization of something I would not have even dreamed of. My prayer continues to be that I make good use of all the tremendous opportunities that the Almighty has so charitably sent my way.

— FRANCIS NATAF
Jerusalem
Kislev 5770

PREFACE

To study Torah is a most difficult undertaking for modern man. It is not the Torah which is the problem but man. To read the text requires courage. Not the courage to open the Book and start reading, but the courage to confront oneself. To learn Torah requires human authenticity, to stand in front of a mirror and ask oneself the devastating question of who one *really* is, without masks and artificialities. And that is one of the qualities modern man has lost. Man has convinced himself to be an intellectual, removed from subjectivity, and to bow only to scientific investigation. As such he has disconnected himself from his self. Because man is a bundle of emotions, passions and subjectivities, he cannot escape – however much he would like to – his inner world. Still modern man "formulates" ideas; he may "proclaim" the rights of the spirit and even "pronounce" laws. But they enter only into his books, into his discussions, but not into his life. All these matters float in mid-air over his head, rather than walk with him into the inner chambers of his daily existence. They do not enter into his trivial moments but stand as monuments, impressive but far removed.

Man is no longer able to struggle with himself about who he is. Therefore he cannot deal with the Biblical text. It stares him in the face and he gets terrified by the confrontation. All that he can do is deny it, escape it so that he can escape himself. Because he knows that he has to come to terms with himself before he comes to terms with the Book, he cannot even negate or disagree with it, as this requires him to deny something that he does not even know exists.

Does that mean that this man is not "religious"? Not at all. Even the religious man is detached from the spirit. He has elevated religion to such a level that its influence on his everyday life in the here and now has been lost. It is found on the top floor with a very special atmosphere of its own. It has been departmentalized. But the meaning of Torah is exactly the reverse. It words, events and commandments are placed in the middle of the people, enveloped in history and worldly matters. What happens there is not taking place in a vacuum but in the hard core of human reality. Most of the Torah deals with the natural course of man's life. Only sporadic moments of miracle tell us about the murmurs of another world which is beyond. These moments remind us that God is, after all, the most real Entity in all of existence. But the Torah is the story of how God exists in the midst of mortal man's regular troubles and joys. It is not the story of God in heaven, but of the God of human history and personal encounter.

My dear friend Rabbi Francis Nataf, Educational Director of the David Cardozo Academy, has once again provided us with penetrating studies about the reality of human existence in the Torah and the great message and relevance of the Biblical stories in our day-to-day life – without allowing us to lose their transcendent meaning. His treatment simultaneously makes us re-enter the minds and hearts of some of the great personalities of the Bible in ways we have previously not considered.

After giving us keen insights in his previous book, *Redeeming Relevance in the Book of Genesis*, this time Rabbi Nataf gives a careful, penetrating look at issues and personalities in the book of Shemot. His analyses are refreshing and most informative and also introduce to us some major elements in Judaism. In his own unique style, Rabbi Nataf has once more done us a great service by engaging us with the words of the Divine text as well as the great Biblical figures without losing sight of the fact that they were human beings who tried to live in the presence of God. For this we are most thankful.

The Cardozo Academy is proud to put out this work.

— RABBI NATHAN LOPES CARDOZO, PH.D.
Dean of The David Cardozo Academy
Machon Ohr Aaron & Betsy Spijer

The Conversation with God

THREE YEARS AFTER its publication, the excitement surrounding the first volume of *Redeeming Relevance* (on Genesis)[1] is still with me. Anticipating a dialogue with my readers, I have found the enthusiastic responses of many of them most gratifying.

Of particular interest is one common response to some of the patterns that I described in the Biblical text. Readers said, "Now that you have pointed it out, I don't know how I could have missed it all this time." This is a typical reaction to many inventions around us. We often don't know what to look for until someone else points it out.

Some of my readers did not notice the patterns that I observed, simply because of how classical texts are taught in most Jewish institutions of learning. While thanks to the efforts of Nechama Leibowitz and her spiritual descendants, countless more classrooms are asking the important educational question, "What's bothering Rashi?", once we figure that out, we are content to simply end our search with Rashi's (or Ramban's or Seforno's) answer and just move on to the next verse. In other words, once we appreciate and understand the question, we are programmed to think that our task is to find its one and only pre-existing answer. We believe that this answer is accessible to all and is the common pursuit of all who embark on the equation.

As a result of this unfortunate perception, that which could serve as an introduction to independent literary analysis becomes more akin to the solving

[1] *Redeeming Relevance in the Book of Genesis* (Jerusalem: Urim Publications, 2006).

of math problems. If for no other reason, the fact that our classical commentators noticed different things and (even when they noticed the same questions) often gave different answers, should make us realize that we are not looking for set answers in the "teacher's edition." Rather, for our commentators, finding a good question in the Divine text served as an invitation for a very *personal* involvement with it, which could not be replicated by anyone else.

Sensitizing ourselves to the types of questions posed and answers given by the greatest Torah exegetes of the past is quite valuable. That type of traditional study allows us to understand "the rules of the game," to appreciate how the Torah speaks to us, to discover which patterns are more significant and which patterns are less so. Without this knowledge, our insights will often remain childish and even boorish. Still, when Rashi studied the text, the questions he asked bothered *him* and the answers that he gave satisfied *him*. It was a personal involvement with the text, and thus *not only an intellectual exercise, but a meaningful religious one as well*; so, too, with all of the great commentaries.

It has been said that when we pray we speak to God, but when we study Torah He speaks to us. But if He is truly speaking to us, what does that entail? If the Torah is God's speech to all Jews, then it is addressed not only to Rashi or Ramban. Many times, God will say the same thing to all of us. But just as what He said to Ramban was often different from what He said to Rashi, we should expect that there will be times when what He will say to us will be different than what He said to either of them.[2] In this way, the *personal* nature of true Torah study is what makes it into an authentic *conversation with God*. It is just such a conversation that is at the center of normative Jewish religious experience.

More important than the specific insights they gave us, then, our great commentators present us with a model of how to approach the text. Among other things, they show us that we need to ask questions that are important to *us* and to discover answers that resonate for *us*. For when we study the Torah only to see what others have said about it, we remove the direct interaction

2   See *Redeeming Relevance in Genesis*, pp. 19–25, on the Torah's use of the same written words to say different things to different audiences.

between Man and God that should be the hallmark of what we call *Talmud Torah*, Torah study.

The Human Language of God

To some, the idea that God talks to us may seem quite astonishing. Indeed, the gap between Man and God is so great that many philosophers have had difficulty coming to terms with the notion of Divine communication with Man in any form. One of the problems is that for God to speak to us He has to speak in our language – we have no other way of understanding concrete and distinct ideas. But how is it that God can limit Himself to the imperfections of human communication? Even if we are to accept the notion that Biblical Hebrew is of Divine origin, its comprehension by Man is automatically imperfect. Moreover, like any living language, even classical Hebrew developed and evolved according to human usage, such that one sees linguistic differences between prophets writing at different times. If so, how can God use the medium of any language, given its imperfection and lack of clarity? But even beyond this, can words ever completely describe the essence of things? We use words because we cannot impart the entire essence of an object or entity to another person, let alone understand that essence ourselves. For God, however, Who does understand the essence of everything, words cannot adequately describe His knowledge of any given entity. But let us leave these problems to the philosophers. Assuming that it is possible for God to speak to us, what type of speech would we expect from Him?

To be sure, human communication encompasses many styles. There is one style we use to give information and another to engender relationship with others. Telling a joke is an example of the latter. But even when it comes to imparting information, though we sometimes just spell things out, we more frequently intersperse information with colorful expressions, body language and the like in order to create a connection between us and the audience. We do this even as we transmit the substantive message that we want to communicate. This is what makes speech interesting. More to the point, it is what makes speech human. Though some of us may claim that we seek only information, rare indeed is the person who would really rather remove the human element and instead listen to a computer tell him what he needs to know.

Thus, since personal communication normally involves connection as well as information, when God decided to communicate with Man, it was certainly enmeshed with the creation of a relationship with human beings.

There are those who see this as an unsustainable example of God's bringing Himself down to our level. In this vein, the Enlightenment philosophers had much less of a problem with God as the Creator of the scientific universe, Who "communicates" with us wordlessly through the mathematical perfection of His creation. They had a harder time with God as the Writer of human words and sentences Who communicates in the way that we ourselves communicate. To them, the "imperfections" of human speech are fine for us, but understandably not for Him Who is perfect.

Such a rational approach makes sense, but it only works as long as God and Man are to stay distant and removed from each other. Although some philosophers preferred this perspective, it led one more devout colleague, Blaise Pascal, to claim that the object of his worship was "the God of Abraham, the God of Isaac, the God of Jacob, not the God of the philosophers and the learned." As Pascal saw it, the God of these philosophers was too removed from the daily affairs of men and accordingly no substitute for the God Whom he knew personally.

Wellhausen or Joyce

On some level, when Bible criticism came to the world with Julius Wellhausen, it came with the assumption that God's authorship of the Bible could be proven or disproven by investigating the book's "scientific" composition. To put it differently, the study of Bible became a science – it could not be studied with other literature in the *human*ities unless its origins were human. (Ironically, only after it became a convention of academic study to assume that the Bible is of human origin could it be studied as literature once again, thereby allowing it to speak in the admittedly *human* way it was meant to speak in the first place.)

Influenced by the prejudices of enlightened Western culture, we may feel some confusion about the Biblical text's seeming imperfection. Not only do some of the stories seem out of chronological order, it is sometimes hard to see any connection between various sections that follow one another. Granted, we are given interesting explanations about the Torah's sequence – for example, the sages famously say that the prohibitions of Shabbat are repeated after the section about building the *Mishkan* (Tabernacle) to teach us that Shabbat takes precedence over the building of the *Mishkan*.[3] Still, such explanations do not completely remove our uneasiness since, like the Bible critics, we also assume that the Torah should be more scientifically organized. We wonder why the Torah couldn't express its teachings in a more straightforward manner. As a result, we become all too cognizant of the Bible critics' underlying contention that the traditional school of reading the Bible is grounded in an artificial desire to forge order out of disorder. They tell us that such an approach can only be the result of submission to dogma at the expense of an objective search for truth.

Unconsciously in agreement with their assumptions, we may be drawn to the Bible critics. After all, they base themselves on a highly rational and reasoned approach. For example, because information appears disorganized, the critics conclude that the Torah combines the writings of various authors into one work. Compiled together, these sources will necessarily overlap and repeat things, etc. Although the compiler's rigor is subject to debate in these circles, the basic premise of multiplicity of texts stands largely unchallenged.

Actually, the whole question of how to look at such issues in the Biblical text is not a uniquely modern one. The Talmud[4] encapsulates the concern through a brief discussion between R. Abahu and an anonymous Sadducee. It is well known that the Sadducees were enamored with Greek (i.e., rational) thought, so it is no coincidence that this one expected the Bible to be in strict chronological order. Hence, when the Sadducee cites an example of the Psalms being out of order, R. Abahu responds by saying that this is only a problem for you (i.e., based on your assumptions). We, however, says R. Abahu, view the order of the Torah as not purely chronological but also associational (*semuchin min haTorah*). Jewish tradition posits that the Torah is organized according to

3 *Mechilta* on *Shemot* 35:1–4.
4 *Berachot* 10a. See also Maharsha ad loc.

the relationship between the content or theme of one section and that which follows it.[5] So, it is not only legitimate for the Torah to be "out of order," it is to be expected. More generally, R. Abahu was suggesting that there really can be order in "disorder."

From the brief Talmudic passage above, it seems that our sages were at least aware of the nexus of the Greek/academic approach to the Bible. It also appears that they basically rejected it as lacking the appropriate paradigms for truly understanding the Bible.

But how should we understand the often elusive order in the disorder? One possible way is by examining a twentieth century literary device called "stream of consciousness." This device, made famous by James Joyce, has the reader follow the thoughts of the protagonist, which often takes him far afield along with the character's thoughts. While more difficult to read, it provides us with an unusually accurate portrayal of human thought. Even as many individual thoughts are quite rational, the connection between one thought and the next is often highly idiosyncratic. The mind flows easily from one subject to another, occasionally in an almost inexplicable fashion. Sometimes one moves on to a thought that is not at all connected to the one that preceded it, but is rather evoked by unconscious stimuli or memories. On some level, this approach to writing is more natural to humanity than a straightforward, chronological rendering of events. After all, we are not just analytical minds – we are complex creatures who reflect upon a tremendous variety of things in all sorts of ways, only some of which even lend themselves to rational investigation.

The lack of consistent chronological order is only one example of the

5   See *Yevamot* 4a, where the Talmud identifies R. Yehudah as someone who believes that we cannot readily determine the meaning of such associations. Even though there are reasons for the order, they are entirely the product of a Divine stream of consciousness which defies our analysis. Thus, R. Yehudah feels we should generally not be looking for connections between one seemingly unrelated section and another proximate one. The opposing opinion tells us that trying to understand the connections between the different parts of this flow of consciousness is a legitimate and productive area of Torah study. This position maintains that we are actually able to arrive at true insights by attempting to understand the Divine stream of consciousness.

Torah's human style of expression. Stream of consciousness – or, better, human communication – is full of inconsistency, subjectivity, disproportionate emphasis and the like. No matter what we want to make of it, it would be hard to deny that the Torah is written with just such a human bent. On some level, this is best expressed by the phrase, appearing many times throughout the Talmud, "The Torah speaks in the language of men."

Modern Man's understandable love affair with scientific methodology can blind him to the fact that human thinking is not naturally scientific. While the scientific method allows us to think clearly and make great material advances, it will always remain divorced from our natural essence. By contrast, it seems that the sages understood that the Biblical text is, and should be, consonant with our *natural mode of thought*, and not with the way we force ourselves to think in the laboratory. The result is that the text speaks in "the language of men" in a way that is organic and that makes the most sense to the inner "I" that the Torah ultimately addresses.

Of course, I am not pretending to be giving a death blow to all Bible criticism in my brief comments above. What I am suggesting, however, is that much of Bible criticism's popularity is based on a subtle paradigm shift that occurred in how to look at the text. If I am correct, it is worth questioning whether this paradigm shift was not, in fact, mistaken.[6]

One of the most brilliant depictions of the conflict between the various approaches to the Bible was shown in the animated film *Lights*. In it, the Greeks were frustrated as they tried to use their scientific instruments to measure Hebrew letters. As opposed to the Greek letters of stone that would sit still and be measured, the Hebrew letters, made of fire and light, were far too active and flexible to endure such treatment.

Indeed, the letters of the Torah cannot "sit still" and so defy scientific analysis. Although our tradition appreciates the role of logic and organization, it does not believe that all of human existence should be understood in such a fashion. At the end of the day, there are limits to what can be measured.

6 Though not directly related, Alisdair MacIntyre raised many an eyebrow not so long ago when he suggested that we reconsider the correctness of the Enlightenment's paradigms shifts in his famous *After Virtue* (Notre Dame: University of Notre Dame Press, 1981).

The entire point of the Torah's manifestly "human" style is to draw us into conversation. But it requires something from us as well. It requires that we hear for ourselves and not through an interpreter. It is certainly useful to study how master "conversationalists" have communicated through the Torah and it is absolutely essential that we learn the language of communication. Otherwise, we merely *react* to sounds or to random words and not to a coherent text that God uses for His conversation with us. Still, this is not the most formidable challenge for those of us who come from the world of traditional Torah study. Instead, our greatest challenge is not to be intimidated by our own smallness in front of the great conversationalists. Equally important is not to be scared by the tremendous weightiness of the task. Like the mountain climber who will lose his balance if he looks down from where he is, the way to achievement in Torah study is to keep looking at the goal – in this case, speaking with God.

Thus, Torah study is the art of listening to God's conversation. He speaks to anyone making a true effort to listen to what the text is saying specifically to him. Of course, that doesn't mean that anyone making an effort will never make a mistake – no more than we never make a mistake when listening to our fellowman, even when we are paying careful attention. What it does mean, however, is that someone who doesn't exert himself to listen has no chance of being involved in this eternal conversation at all.

This is the living experience of *Talmud Torah* and presumably the type of activity for which we bless God every morning. When all is said and done, all of our conversations with each other are just practice for the existential act of listening to God's voice.

In this volume, I invite the reader to my conversations with Eternity.

CHAPTER I

The Cradle and the Crucible:
The Meaning of Egypt

FOR THE LAND TO WHICH YOU ARE GOING . . . *is not like the land of Egypt* . . . it is a land of hills and valleys, from the rain of the skies it drinks water. It is a land that *Hashem*, your God inspects; the eyes of *Hashem*, your God, are constantly upon it, from the beginning of the year until the end of the year. (*Devarim* 11:10–12)

IF THE FIRST book of the Torah starts with the creation of the world, the second book begins with another genesis, the creation of the Jewish people.[1] At the beginning of *Shemot*, the Torah's second book, we see the fateful arrival of Ya'akov's large and distinguished family in the land of Egypt. It is there that we read about this family becoming a nation.

Like the initial genesis of the world, the creation of the Jewish people is not just about proliferation. The history of the Jews in Egypt is the story of the creation of a distinctive identity that would create a new consciousness among the descendents of Ya'akov. How this nation came into being is obviously of great import. Yet the Torah gives us only a basic outline of the process. This is

---

1   Indeed, it has been suggested that there are important parallels between the early development of mankind and the early development of the Jewish people. I first heard this idea from my friend and colleague, Rabbi Nathaniel Helfgot, who subsequently pointed out that others have also made this comparison. See, for example, Amos Chacham, *Da'at Mikra – Shemot* (Jerusalem: Mossad haRav Kook, 1991), p. 16.

very much in keeping with the terse, nuanced Biblical style, which demands careful reading and skillful interpretation to arrive at its full meaning.

In studying the birth of the Jewish nation, we immediately ponder the significance of the story's geographical location and whether the foundational experiences of the Jewish people could not have happened elsewhere. In other words, is the fact that this national genesis occurred in Egypt ultimately co-incidental or does it add an important dimension to the future shape of the Jewish nation? To address such a question, we will need to look at what the Torah tells us about the land of our national origins, a land that would ironi-cally become the paradigm of all future oppressors of the holy nation to which it gave birth.

What Is Egypt?

It is certainly no coincidence that Egypt is mentioned a great deal in the Bible. In fact, it appears almost seven hundred times. Besides Israel, which is under-standably mentioned more than Egypt, the next runner-up, Babylonia, is men-tioned only about two hundred and fifty times. If nothing else, this statistic reveals the Bible's fascination with Israel's western neighbor.

Egypt's proximity and its resultant political and military influence over Israel makes its centrality expected. At the same time, the relationship be-tween the Jews and Egypt is much more involved than what is necessitated by mere geopolitics. We might say that classical Jewish culture has a fixation on Egypt.

Egypt serves as a constant place of refuge from famine and conquest, yet it is the *only* place where Jews are Biblically prohibited to live.[2] That the Jews in the Bible nonetheless continue to be more connected to Egypt than to anywhere else only serves to create depth as well as irony to the Torah's pro-hibition. This country is somehow friend *and* foe – often at the same time. Whatever it is, however, its intertwining with the Jewish nation reinforces our desire to understand what Egypt is all about.

2   *Devarim* 17:16.

What does the Torah tell us about the geographical entity we call Egypt? First of all, Egypt functions as a place of economic refuge for those living around it. Both Avraham and Ya'akov go to Egypt when confronted with famine.[3] Yitzchak would have done the same had he not been prohibited by special Divine mandate.[4] Moreover, we read that other nations would also come to Egypt to find sustenance in times of famine.[5] Were we to know nothing else, these passages immediately show us that even when the rest of the region is experiencing drought, Egypt is somehow spared.

In fact, the fidelity and bounty of Egyptian agriculture is only further brought out by its descriptions in the Torah. The first reference, early on in the book of *Bereshit*, which compares Egypt to God's garden,[6] says it all: from a certain perspective, this land is idyllic. The basis for this perspective is explained further in the book of *Devarim*, where we read that Egyptian agriculture does not require much physical effort.[7] Still another reference tells us that pots full of meat were available even to the slaves there.[8] Accordingly, not only is the land easy to work, it also produces great bounty.

Even without the Torah's descriptions, it is well-known that the Nile River would regularly overflow its banks, creating dependable fertility throughout the whole area. In turn, the agricultural plenty this created allowed Egypt to amass its famous power and wealth, attested to by the great treasures and monuments it left over for all generations to see until this very day.

In turn, Egypt's wealth allowed it to develop a military capability that afforded it physical security, a commodity unknown to most other nations in the area. The Land of Israel, for example, was constantly fighting with its immediate neighbors as well as trying to escape the wrath of the major empires. Although Egypt also had to contend with the rival empires that would arise every few hundred years, nonetheless, as opposed to God's chosen people next

3   *Bereshit* 12:10 and 46:6, respectively.

4   Ibid., 26:1–2.

5   Ibid., 41:57.

6   Ibid., 13:10.

7   *Devarim* 11:10.

8   *Shemot* 16:3.

door, most Egyptians did not need to constantly worry about being attacked by the likes of the Philistines or the Moabites!

Mitzrayim, Son of Cham

One might think that such a fortunate situation would be given to a nation that God favors. At the very least, one might expect this situation to create an intense religious gratitude to the spiritual forces responsible for such tranquility. As we will discover, this is not at all what the Torah saw. And not only did the Torah not see this, it also wanted to make sure that the reader would not even *entertain* such a perspective.

The land and people of Egypt (Mitzrayim) were named after its ancestor, the son of Cham and the grandson of Noach. As is generally known, Cham is the least illustrious of Noach's children. This comes out most clearly after the flood subsides and human inhabitation of the earth begins anew.⁹ At that time, when Noach gets drunk, Cham doesn't help his father in the same way as Shem and Yefet do. Moreover, though it remains unclear exactly what Cham did when he saw his father naked, it was enough to cause Noach to curse him (through his son Cana'an), instead of bless him as he did his two other sons.¹⁰ A simple reading of the text shows that when Cham saw his father naked, rather than cover him he went to tell his brothers. The Midrash suggests that his behavior was much more depraved,¹¹ a reading for which one can find hints in the Biblical text. Yet even the simple narrative ascertains that Cham did not know how to respond appropriately to his father's nakedness.

Since the Torah commonly considers a person's descendents to be highly influenced by him (all the more so when we are talking about the father of a nation or nations), if Cham's weakness lay in sexual depravity, we would not be surprised if the same were true of his progeny. In fact, the Torah gives us several indications that it views ancient Egypt as a nation marked by sexual

---

9   *Bereshit* 9:18–29.
10 While it is not exactly blessings that Noach gives Shem and Cham, certainly when compared to his treatment of Cham, it would be fair here to refer to them as blessings.
11 *Sanhedrin* 70a.

immorality. The clearest reference to this is when Avraham feels a need for special precautions to protect his marriage with Sarah *specifically* in Egypt.[12] We conclude from this that so voracious was the Egyptians' lust and so little did they value human life that Avraham fully expected his new neighbors to ignore the most basic natural law to satisfy their desires – i.e., to murder him in order to get to his wife.

The story of Yosef and Potiphar's wife a bit later shows that Avraham was not just imagining the problem. From her unusually forward advances, we note that even the women in Egypt were willing to blatantly ignore fundamental moral conventions when engaged in the pursuit of sexual gratification. Taking its cue from these and other Scriptural passages, rabbinic tradition further expands on the theme of Egyptian depravity in rather colorful fashion.[13] Thus, when the Bible specifically refers to Egypt, as opposed to any of the other descendant nations of Cham, as *the land of Cham*, it appears to be emphasizing the ancestral roots of this particular people's depravity.[14] In that case, Cham's Egyptian descendents serve as an antithesis to the moral *tikkun olam* that God would want the Jews to bring to the world.

◆ ◆ ◆

Now that we know more about the Biblical view of the Egyptians, we clearly see that when it comes to Egypt, the Torah purposefully portrays a naturally inverse relationship between Divine bounty on the one hand and human virtue on the other.

God wants all of His creatures, including the ancient Egyptians, to live moral and upstanding lives. Nonetheless, He still allows them to follow their own paths. The rabbis say that God actually helps a person accomplish whatever he wants to accomplish, whether good or bad.[15] Accordingly, if the Egyptian nation were interested in moral depravity, God would presumably equip them to accomplish their goals.

12 *Redeeming Relevance in Genesis*, pp. 67–68.
13 See, for example, *Midrash Tanchuma,* Parashat Lech Lecha 5 and *Mechilta* 13 on *Shemot* 12:33.
14 *Tehillim* 105:23, 27; 106:22.
15 *Makkot* 10b.

One of the means that God could use to push us further in the path we have chosen for ourselves is situating us in an environment that will support and even encourage the behavior we are pursuing. The most important component of this is the human landscape of the people who surround us. At the same time, our non-human, physical environment also impacts upon our behavior. To give one example, it is recognized that weather affects crime rates – if for no other reason, inclement weather keeps people indoors and prevents them from hurting others.

Another very common determinant is whether a given region is more suitable for farming than for raising livestock or hunting. From the very first family, the Torah understands that these various pursuits will impact on more than just culinary habits. At the same time, even the latter should not be overlooked as contributing to our ethical makeup – some commentators have suggested that a type of "you are what you eat" concept is what makes certain animals kosher and others not.[16] Most of these variables were even more exacerbated in the ancient world when exportation of food was much less common and climate control almost non-existent. Hence, conditions beyond man's control can actually raise or lower a nation's moral standards.

All this being the case, we would expect the Egyptians to be given a land inhospitable to moral and religious growth. That is to say, it would be appropriate for God to give a metaphysically dull land to the spiritually listless Egyptians[17] – quite the opposite of the "garden of God" that they received. Moreover, the Torah goes out of its way to point out the close relationship between this people and their land in much the same way as it does with the Jewish people and their land, giving us the distinct impression that we have to think further about how the blessed Egyptian garden may be much less desirable than first meets the eye.

---

16 See, especially, Rabbi S. R. Hirsch in *Chorev*, Chapter 68.

17 An obvious question that this approach would raise is why the equally immoral Cana'anite descendents of Cham should have been the caretakers of the spiritually productive Land of Israel before they were spit out from it.

The Land and Its People

Having just mentioned the Torah's parallel interest in the relationship between the Jewish people and *its* land, it behooves us to see how that interest
is grounded in the text's very deliberate contrast of the lands of Israel and
Egypt.[18] As opposed to Egypt, the Torah informs us that the Land of Israel
is dependent on rains, a highly variable and unpredictable commodity in the
semi-arid Middle East. From a material point of view, a farmer is certainly
much better off in Egypt. The Torah immediately continues its description
by telling us that the irregularity of rains is indicative of constant Divine involvement in this land's sustenance. In the words of the Torah, "God's eyes are
constantly upon it." Here too, it is not so obvious that this makes it a more
desirable place to live. Indeed, it is not just the farmer who might prefer to
live elsewhere, without the pressures that God's direct oversight would likely
entail.

In addition to the issues explicitly stated above, there is another natural
difficulty with this land which the Torah doesn't mention outright[19] – its geo-
political location. Israel finds itself on the only land bridge between Africa and
Eurasia. Anyone and, more important, any army that would want to go from
one continent to the other would have to pass through it, or at least very close
to it. As such, it doesn't have the luxury of a Yemen or a Norway, tucked away
in its own little corner and able to ignore the world. It is true that Egypt was
on the other side of this land bridge and subsequently subject to some of the
same issues. Still, Egypt had the military power to deter any potential threats
created by such a situation. For the weaker Jewish state, however, the only
thing that might protect it was . . . the eyes of God constantly upon it.

The same wonder that we had about God's giving Egypt to its inhabitants
comes up with Israel and its inhabitants. Why is this dangerous, uncertain
place the type of land that God wants to give to the Chosen People – the ones
He describes as his firstborn?

18 *Devarim* 11:10–12 (quoted at the beginning of this chapter).
19 Although a careful reading of all the Biblical wars and political conflicts forced on
Israel as a result of its geographical location would certainly bear this out – as would
a reading of regional history in general.

If we look a bit deeper into the contrast set up, we will see that Israel's portion is a true blessing. The contrast that emerges between the lands of Israel and Egypt is primarily between a place that lacks *natural* resources and one that doesn't. Precisely a land that lacks such resources requires God's attention. Put plainly, something fragile and needy requires more interest than something solid and self-sustaining. Though we just questioned whether anyone would want such potentially overwhelming attention, from a spiritual perspective it is that which gives the most meaning to life. And for someone truly interested in God, this is worth the collateral loss of physical stability.

As opposed to the indulgence the Egyptians could ascribe to their gods, who would feed and protect them no matter what they did, the Jews had a vision of God constantly watching them while deciding how much bounty and security they would deserve in any particular year. If nothing else, this would encourage the Jews to do what God commanded them. But it appears that it did more than this. The prophets and the religious tradition that they handed over to the rabbis bespeaks a nation whose consciousness was saturated with God's presence and the accompanying importance of acting in a way that reflects man's Divine image. If the Nile generally seemed to validate the "watchmaker" concept of a God Who sets things into motion and no longer needs to intervene, Israel's dependence on irregular rainfall gave truth to the model of a God continually involved with His creations. The Jews would eventually understand the need to be challenged and thus appreciate what their land did for them.

For their part, the Egyptians too, with their sensual appetites, were likely just as happy with what their land did (or in this case, did not do) for them. We now see that it is more than predisposition that led the Egyptians to follow their indulgent lifestyle; their relative prosperity and security further enabled them to treat religion as a matter of convenience. When a person's life or livelihood hangs in the balance, he is much more able to realize his dependence on forces beyond his control. In marked contrast, security allows one to ignore not only one's latent faith, but also one's moral conscience. Without an awareness of consequences, most people simply have an easier time indulging in behavior they know to be wrong. And in this regard, Egypt could be seen as a land free of consequences.

◆ ◆ ◆

Though much more can be said, we have emerged with some general contours of the Torah's view of Egypt. It was a land of plenty that both attracted and encouraged the moral mediocrity of its inhabitants. It served as a sort of alter ego for the Land of Israel, whose unpredictability led to the religious introspection and self-critique so characteristic of the Jewish prophetic tradition. With this as our foundation, let us now try to understand the constant involvement of the Jews themselves with Egypt. Most directly, why should this land have served as the crucible within which the Jewish nation was formed?

Leaving Egypt

Happiness is a tricky proposition. To be sure, much of both our lives and human history is dedicated to its pursuit, which involves, among other things, efforts to improve our physical condition. Since it is God Who has given us the potential and even the directive to do so, it is perfectly legitimate for man to try to earn a stable and comfortable livelihood. At the same time, the inverse relationship between bounty and morality seen above is also part of the way we are created. The famous warning Moshe gives to the Jews that *va'yishman Yeshurun va'yiv'at* (When the Jews got fat, they rebelled)[20] is a graphic expression of that relationship. Even as God wants us to maximize our benefit from His creation, He also wants us to seek such benefit only in ways that don't compromise our spiritual health. Meeting this challenge is an important part of the Jewish vision.[21]

In order to take on this challenge, the Jews had to be impressed by the temptations of prosperity. Were they to be divorced from any material ambitions, they would never fully know the important human tension between spirituality and physicality.

In this regard, Ya'akov's family's coming to Egypt as brothers of the obviously privileged viceroy certainly provided immediate exposure to the

20 *Devarim* 32:15.
21 See *Redeeming Relevance in Genesis*, Chapter 5.

29

ostensible benefits of Egyptian culture. From the get-go, they would be surrounded by the wealth and splendor of Pharaoh. And if royalty is always impressive, there was certainly nothing as magnificent in the ancient world as the glory of the Egyptian court. The preferential treatment they received afforded them the best that Egypt's wealth had to offer and allowed them to be wholly impressed by the regular bounty of Egypt.

But it may have been something more sober than surplus and luxury that would have impressed Ya'akov and sons: The ability of the Egyptian governmental organization to overcome a pan-regional famine must have had a particularly heightened impact on men who had recently felt their own helplessness in the face of scarcity. It should be recalled that the long-delayed decision to send Binyamin to Egypt came only as a result of Ya'akov's realization that they would otherwise die of starvation. The notion of Egypt as a land blessed by nature, to the point that rational planning was the only thing needed to make sure that all of its inhabitants would be sustained, is certainly attractive for those who have known starvation in more arid lands. Thus, even more than a land of plenty, Egypt would be seen as a land of economic stability.

Once impressed, however, the Jews' destiny would require that they extricate themselves from Egyptian culture and even reject it. In other words, the point was not, after admiring the wealth of Egypt, to simply adopt the moral lethargy of the local culture. Instead, the Jews would have to truly appreciate the spiritual challenges of wealth and yet still somehow overcome them.

Just such an attitudinal change was facilitated by the change in Egyptian policy toward the Jews. The group that had arrived as honored guests was to be made into a caste of slaves. Once ostracized from Egyptian society, the Jews could afford to be more critical of the host culture – they no longer had any reason to look the other way in the face of Egypt's moral turpitude and cruelty.

The Exodus itself was another major step in extricating the Jews from that which Egypt represented. Had they not yet completely appreciated the immorality of Egyptian culture, the unprecedented Divine wrath unleashed during the Exodus must have made a very big impression indeed. The Jews surely understood that the plagues inflicted on Egypt were a barometer of God's opinion of the nation's values. Indeed, the very first, and arguably most dramatic of the plagues was meted out against the Nile – the very symbol of

Egyptian wealth, stability and self-reliance. Allegiance to the God of the ten plagues would now more clearly mean rejection of Egypt.

But it would take more than Egyptian oppression and the resultant Exodus to completely rid the Jews of their attraction to the stability and materialism they had once enjoyed. The struggles with food,[22] with gold and with jewelry[23] that would continue to plague them in the desert show that the extraction from Egyptian indulgence, and the religious stance that it spawned, was a process which did not completely end when the Jews left Egypt. Accepting the disadvantages of physical instability in order to reap spiritual benefits is no small undertaking. Accordingly, the Jews' latent attachment to Egypt's constancy goes far toward explaining their recurring reluctance to enter the Promised Land, as well as their constant refrain of wanting to return to Egypt.

This resistance is further epitomized by some of the Jews' strangely identifying *Egypt* as the land flowing with milk and honey,[24] a phrase more commonly used to refer to the Land of Israel. It is also epitomized by the spies' reference to the Promised Land as a land that eats up its inhabitants.[25] Beyond resistance to new vistas, such declarations would now also bespeak rebellion against God Who, by taking the Jews out of Egypt, was calling them to meet their spiritual destiny. As a result, once the Jews left Egypt, being a Jew became synonymous with the struggle to remove "Egypt" from within oneself. The Exodus from Egypt would signal a continual struggle to accept at least some instability as the price for heightened spirituality. Indeed, though the Jews got out of Egypt, the struggle to get Egypt out of the Jews has continued for much of Jewish history.

Notwithstanding the continuous internal struggle just described, the antagonistic position toward Egyptian culture that the Jews consolidated as things came to a head in Egypt also allowed them to make a decisive break from that culture. It helped them realize that it would be more advantageous

22 See, for example, *Bemidbar* 11:4–10.
23 The prominent role of jewelry in the construction of the golden calf leads the rabbis (*Berachot* 32a) to make the claim that the Jews would have been better off leaving such items in Egypt.
24 *Bemidbar* 16:13.
25 Ibid., 13:32.

to leave stability behind. This would be a major precondition to their ability to go back to the tumultuous land of their fathers. [26]

A Land of Extremes

> We came to the land to which you sent us and it is truly a land flowing with milk and honey and this is its fruit. But the people that live in the land are fierce and the cities are very strongly fortified . . . it is a land that eats up its inhabitants. (*Bemidbar* 13:27–28, 32)

Given what we have discussed so far, the notion that the Land of Israel would be a harsh place to live should be fully expected. Accordingly, it is quite possible, as claimed by Ramban, that the spies who were sent to scout out the Promised Land and came back with a critical report did not lie.[27] It is truly a land of extremes – having bountiful fruit on the one hand and consuming its inhabitants on the other – and living there is no simple matter. As expressed elsewhere in the Torah,[28] the Land of Israel is more than unstable; it is sometimes downright hostile.[29]

More difficult to understand is how the Torah could also describe this land as flowing with milk and honey (an association confirmed above by the scouts, who were probably not looking to paint the land in glowing terms). To say that it *flows* indicates a lack of human effort, reminiscent more of Egypt than of Israel. How are we to understand that the Land of Israel could flow with anything – much less with sweet and rich foods? And how are we further to explain this in view of what we said before, that this land seemed to give its inhabitants only the sustenance merited by their behavior?

---

26 The rejection of Egyptian materialism could additionally provide a novel explanation as to why the Jews may not have been eager to take the gold and silver that God told them to request from the Egyptians (see *Berachot* 9a-b). It was a reminder of the part of Egypt that they were specifically rejecting via the Exodus.

27 Ramban on *Bemidbar* 13:27.

28 See, for example, *Vayikra* 18:28.

29 This is in order to destroy the morally corrupt people who dwell in it. Thus, even this consuming of inhabitants that the spies believed to be the Land of Israel's shortcoming could actually be seen as an additional dimension of its praise.

In fact, we will need to refine our original analysis. We saw that the Land of Israel responds to the behavior of its inhabitants, but we now see that it does so in a surprisingly extreme way. The unusually large fruits[30] reflect that the Land provides *exponential* rewards for the merit achieved by its inhabitants.[31] At the same time, inhabitants could expect much swifter and more complete retribution for their sins than would be the case elsewhere. In sum, when the Land of Israel's inhabitants live according to the land's rules, they are given not only what they need, but much more. When they do not, they bear a disproportionate punishment. If this doesn't meet the conventional view of objective reward and punishment, it does remind us of a father extremely concerned about properly raising his only son. From this perspective, we could say that the Land of Israel responds to its inhabitants with a type of parental wisdom and care.

Ultimately, however, the scouts' description of the land only reinforces the impressions we have until now – that Israel is a land of fluctuating extremes, which is another way of saying instability. As opposed to Egypt, which was the epitome of agricultural constancy, Israel was a land of volatility, providing almost effortless bounty to some inhabitants and being barren to others. Yet, in different ways, both lands could be described as *flowing* with milk and honey. The difference is that whereas in the Land of Israel the flow brings more spirituality, in Egypt it does the opposite.

Common Spirituality

Ideally, we should be able to focus on spiritual matters, regardless of what is around us. Whether we are in "Israel" or in "Egypt" and no matter what our personal needs, we should seek connection with God. Indeed, a great figure

---

30 As indicated by the context of their presentation. The scouts praise the land before they show the fruit, and it is only afterward that they begin their next statement with the oppositional word, "however."

31 The Cana'anite inhabitants are not described as particularly upstanding. Still, that is not to say that they never did meritorious acts for which they could have been rewarded. Moreover, this would be in line with the rabbinic notion that evil people get whatever reward is coming to them in the physical realm and not in the spiritual realm (see, for example, Rashi on *Kiddushin* 39b, s.v. *matnitin*).

such as Moshe was able to reach the heights of spirituality outside of Israel. Nonetheless, our rabbis were quite aware that very few people are like him; most people are not able to serve God without any expectations of His fulfilling their needs. Thus, the rabbis' highly practical formulation of the standard *shemoneh esreh* prayer – the backbone of the Jewish daily service – is based on the notion that one who doesn't focus on real needs is not likely to seek God at all.[32]

The common man is down-to-earth. He fills his time with what he must do to survive and flourish. If he doesn't have rain for his crops, he has to do something about it. In the Land of Israel, doing something means turning to God. In Egypt, such a situation rarely comes up, which means that turning to God is a luxury for which the Egyptian "has no time." Thus, in the Land of Israel, it is the common man who has the most to gain.

Since God is interested in the heightened spirituality of the entire Jewish nation and not merely its exceptional individuals, there needs to be a supportive physical environment. That environment is the Promised Land . . . of Israel.

◆　◆　◆

The Exodus from Egypt serves as an important model of going from an inner exile to an inner redemption on a very *accessible* level. The Jews needed to experience how material stability can threaten their communion with God.[33] First experiencing the draw of material comfort in Egypt meant that they would always know its power. Eventually seeing the opposite in the Land of Israel meant they would forever accept the need to prioritize spirituality. The challenging process of making the transition from one to the other, symbolized by the journey through the desert, is destined to be the struggle of the common man who seeks to live his life in front of God.

◆　◆　◆

32　So too can we understand the curious wording of the blessing said after minor foods, where we thank God not only for fulfilling our needs but also for creating our physical lacks to begin with.

33　That their relationship with God had deteriorated in Egypt is confirmed in *Yechezkel* 20:5–8. See also Seforno on *Shemot* 1:13–14 and Rabbi S. R. Hirsch on *Shemot* 1:9.

Can one live outside of Israel and still live his life in accordance with the land's teachings? Conversely, is living in Israel enough to guarantee an approach to life that is fostered by this land? Moreover, today, when rainfall is less crucial to our sustenance, is there still a significant distinction between Israel and other places that have more reliable sources of water?

If globalization has certainly diminished geographical differentiation, Israel remains a uniquely unpredictable place. The return of the Jews to their homeland, intended by the state's founders to bring greater security to the Jews, has been accompanied by constant conflict. Security is actually only one of a whole list of issues that keeps life in Israel more than a bit unpredictable. Whether this will change before the messianic era we cannot know.

Nonetheless, it would be hard to say that the life of the Jew in Israel today is more unstable than the life of the Jew in the Diaspora for the last two thousand years. Facing one expulsion after another in addition to every type of persecution imaginable, the Jews' existence outside of their land was at least every bit as precarious as that in their own land. It is as if once the Jews came out of Egypt, their fate would be to live a "Land of Israel" type of existence no matter where they settled.

At the same time, the rational organization and distribution of resources by the modern welfare state is specifically aimed at, among other things, the creation of stability for its inhabitants. Like all such states, modern Israel has been working hard to provide bounty and security for its inhabitants and, on many fronts, it is succeeding. As such, whether within or outside of Israel, the contemporary Jew knows more stability today than he has in a very long time.

The fact that modern society has been able to do much to push away life's precariousness is a blessing, but it can easily turn into a curse as well. Since we now see that instability can be very productive religiously, we should not be so quick to make our lives so comfortable. In making personal life choices, we can usually take the safest option available. However, this should not always be seen as the wisest option. Beyond making for a rather dull and unfulfilled life, it can end up distancing us from God.

I am certainly not advocating that we act carelessly, flaunting the responsibilities that properly ordered lives require. Still, we should welcome a certain amount of risk in our lives. For most of us, it is exactly that characteristic embodied by the Land of Israel that leads us to seek God.

Minimally, if we have become too soft to take the risks usually needed for intense religiosity, we must make sure to find an alternative strategy that will allow us to achieve the same ends. Otherwise, the most significant religious result of the modern state may end up as *va'yishman Yeshurun* . . .

CHAPTER 2

Moshe's Stutter: The Pardonable Sin

NEAR THE BEGINNING of the book of *Shemot*, we meet a larger-than-life personality. Moshe, the Torah's main human actor, truly defies the limits of humanness, or more precisely, shows us that there are no such limits, short of becoming God Himself. As Moshe is so different from us it is difficult to say anything definitive about him. At the same time, his immense presence demands our attention.

If we are to gain any insight at all into Moshe, it would likely come from an analysis of his early formative years, a time when his life experience more closely replicates our own. (Even though his youth could hardly be described as typical, it is still within the realm of the recognizable.) Perhaps it is for this reason that the Torah presents a more detailed picture of these years.

In the early chapters about Moshe, we are treated to one of the most fascinating and revealing narratives about any individual in the Torah. Through Moshe's first interview with God, we are able to see his personality, before he takes on his role as God's closest confidant. The highly unusual dialogue gives us an important glimpse of the transition from Moshe's earlier years to his more mature period when he has already been elevated to become God's central prophet.

On some level, Moshe's first dialogue with God sets the tone not only for Moshe's religious life but for the Jewish tradition as a whole. With this in mind, we might have expected the scene at the burning bush to be full of religious consecration and bliss. Instead, we are confronted with discord and disagreement, as the striking main feature of the story here is Moshe's arguing with God.

Moshe presumably learned that it was proper to argue with God from his own family tradition about Avraham, who most famously mounted a vigorous defense of the wicked city of Sodom. Still, the scene at the burning bush is informingly distinctive. It is different from what we see in Avraham's arguments in both content and tone. It is equally different from the more mature Moshe's arguments when he would defend the Jewish people time after time before God. At the burning bush, Moshe is particularly unyielding, refusing God's call to assume national leadership. In fact, given that it is God with Whom he is arguing, his behavior seems out-and-out audacious. Furthermore, as this is Moshe's first reported prophecy, we would expect him to be just the opposite: more cautious and less assertive.

Moshe's arguing with God could be attributed to the reticence of many Jewish leaders upon their initiation to office. In my volume on *Bereshit*, I argued that heightened ambivalence about leadership is a trademark of true Jewish leaders.[1] Nonetheless, with Moshe it goes beyond the reluctance common to the others. And if his attempts to avoid the Divine calling are truly *sui generis*, it is likely that his motivation is *sui generis* as well and needs to be examined on its own merits. In order to do this, we will presently take a more careful look at the introductory exchange between God and Moshe.

The Stubborn Speech Impediment

Moshe repeatedly (and as a result, revealingly) says that his speech impediment prevents him from carrying out God's mandate. God's answer[2] seems so obvious that one wonders why Moshe had not been embarrassed to even bring it up. It is manifestly clear that God is able to fix Moshe's speech if it is necessary.[3] We take it for granted that God knows what He is doing when He asks Moshe to be an emissary to Pharaoh. The obviousness of the answer and

---

1   *Redeeming Relevance in Genesis*, pp. 114–16.
2   *Shemot* 4:11.
3   For this reason, some commentators try to explain Moshe's claim in ways that attempt to avoid this problem.

Moshe's multiple repetition of the problem even after hearing God's response[4] tell us to dig deeper. Indeed, the text mandates that we look below the surface.

Moshe cannot seem to get over the limitations that his impediment creates for him. He seems to be obsessed with it. The difficulty in understanding Moshe's seeming obstinacy about this point makes us believe that the speech impediment represents something much deeper than a specific physical limitation. It seems to be – at least from Moshe's perspective – part of his core identity, and therefore would not be subject to change. It would be part of Moshe's essence even if God were to take away the actual physical defect. To put it differently, Moshe didn't merely think that he had a speech impediment: on some level, he felt that he *was* a speech impediment. He internalized its implications so deeply that it took on essential personal meaning. What we need to know now is why Moshe felt so intimately connected with his defect.

A physical impediment drives home the idea that we humans are not in complete control of our most basic functions. Thus, Moshe's speech impediment serves as a manifestation of his intrinsic human imperfection. Like anyone else – and regardless of his speech impediment – he was imperfect simply as a result of being human. The only difference between Moshe and others is that Moshe's humility made him constantly and intensely aware of his inevitable limitations. Consequently, he felt that he could never properly represent God – especially to the most powerful and grandiose man alive. For this reason, Moshe raises and repeats the problem of his speech impediment *specifically* concerning his mission to Pharaoh.

There are other places, especially in rabbinic literature, where Moshe's humanness is discussed in similar fashion. One famous vignette is Moshe being verbally attacked by the angels, who claim that by virtue of his being a man and not an angel he should be ineligible to receive the Torah.[5] If Moshe expresses

4 *Shemot* 6:12, 30. According to some commentators, these two verses are actually reporting the same incident (see, for example, Rashi). Others note that the phrasing of the second verse, i.e., that Moshe is speaking "in front of God" rather than "to God" is a way of saying that Moshe is really muttering to himself rather than confronting God with this same claim once again (see, for example, Rabbi S. R. Hirsch and Ohr haChaim). Regardless, the very fact that the Torah reviews this unusual and previously defeated argument is certainly worth noting.

5 *Shabbat* 88b.

his concern about a mortal representing God to Pharaoh, the rabbis suggest that this concern is even more in place when it comes to Moshe's ultimate task – that of bringing God's will down to mankind.

In the Torah itself, Moshe's humanness invites challenge from his fellow-men, allowing them to question the purity of his motivations.[6] Even his own brother and sister accuse him of misunderstanding the personal implications of his prophecy.[7] That particular episode is only one of a list of events wherein Moshe's judgment is questioned. It is hard to imagine such doubts on the part of the Jews had the leadership been entrusted to an angel; and all the more so, to God Himself.[8] It is the palpable public awareness of Moshe's humanness that made him vulnerable to attack.

Hence, we see that since Moshe is to reach higher than anyone else, being human is a real issue. He is keenly aware that his incomparable stature is compromised by this fact. And that awareness is encapsulated in Moshe's obsession with his speech impediment. Ultimately, it is his way of saying, "I can't see how this (i.e., a human communicating God's will) can be done."

From this perspective, when Moshe asks God to send someone else,[9] he isn't saying that there would be another *person* better qualified than he. Rather, the task of representing God should be given over to God Himself or at least to angels, as had usually been the case up until now.[10] God's glory and perfection could be represented only by another perfect being.[11]

An alternative understanding of Moshe's request is that he wanted God to give the task of representing Him to a human being less concerned about the precarious nature of the charge, someone less aware of his own human imperfection. This could be compared to a skyscraper window-washer – too much awareness of his situation would paralyze him.

---

6   See, for example, Korach's claims that Moshe's leadership was based on personal vested interests, in *Bemidbar* 16:3.

7   *Bemidbar* 12:1–2.

8   Though we know that the Jews in the desert were not entirely beyond this either.

9   *Shemot* 4:13.

10   Both suggestions can be found in *Shemot Rabba* (3:4 and 3:16 respectively).

11   Indeed, the highly popular rabbinic tradition that Moshe would eventually reach the level of angels and shed all of his physical needs could be seen as a modified expression of this idea.

Of Greatness and Humility

At first glance, it may seem paradoxical for mankind's greatest prophet to be so fixated on his human frailty – one would think that the fewer the imperfections, the easier it would be to overlook them. Yet our astonishment only reveals how warped our own perspective is. Warped, that is, in an ultimate sense, as we shall explain.

We rarely examine how we look at time and space – most of us think that ten years is a long time and ten minutes is a short time. Likewise, we think of a mouse as a small animal and an elephant as a large one. We take for granted that this is a universally true viewpoint. If we were to think more carefully, we would realize that from an ant's perspective a mouse is really quite large and from a whale's perspective an elephant is rather average. Once we understand that the human perspective is a relative one, taking for granted that humans are at the center of all existence, we get greater insight into Moshe. As Moshe grew to have a more refined understanding of God, he likely started leaving his human viewpoint behind and looking at the world from God's perspective. From such a point of view, a man is very small indeed.

At the end of Moshe's life, the Torah tells us that he was the greatest prophet who ever lived.[12] Based on the Torah's description of his giant stature, it is likely that Moshe knew of his greatness throughout his prophetic career. What allowed Moshe to have this awareness and still be, as the Torah reports, the most humble of all men, was his perspective: If a great person compares himself to other humans, he will think very highly of himself. If, however, he sees himself from the vantage point of God – as Moshe's fixation on his imperfection would indicate – he would feel quite small. To put if differently, even if you are the greatest ant in the world, how great can an ant be? True, man is far superior to an ant on many different levels. Still, it would be difficult to claim that the difference between man and ants is greater than the difference between man and God.

It follows, then, that the greatest man was also the most humble. True hu-

---

12 *Devarim* 34:1.

41

mility comes from an elevated and ultimately truer stance – one which forces us to be conscious of our intrinsic imperfection.

The Argument that God "Lost"

Before we return to Moshe's humility, we should turn our attention to other peculiarities about God's argument with Moshe. To begin with, after God has debunked every excuse Moshe presents, Moshe amazes us by basically saying, "I just won't do it."[13] Left with no reason to refuse, his insistence is hard to understand. And instead of God rebuking him, it looks as if He partially gives in. In this apparent compromise, God gives over the public side of leadership to Moshe's brother, Aharon.[14] This, according to tradition, marks the end of an *entire week* of arguing with God.[15] Moreover, even after Moshe accepts the compromise, he repeats his old excuse of having a speech problem only a few chapters later.[16] Even after accepting his task, Moshe clearly remains doubtful about his eligibility for the job.

God appears to appreciate His prophets' arguing with Him in certain situations.[17] But even so, we never see a prophet saying, "I disagree even if I have no reason for it." Such an argument would be audacious in front of any interlocutor, all the more so in front of the Master of the Universe. God's unexpected response to Moshe begs comparison with His more conventional one when confronted with the refusal of the prophet Yonah to carry out his charge.[18] Yonah's refusal to obey results in personal ordeals and, in the end, he

13 See Abarbanel on *I Shmuel* 16:2 who understands Moshe's reluctance in *Shemot* 6:12 in this way as well.
14 *Shemot* 4:14–16.
15 *Yerushalmi, Berachot* 9:7.
16 *Shemot* 6:12.
17 See my unpublished essay entitled, "Herzl, Chutzpah and Heresy," archived at www.cardozoschool.org.
18 *Yonah* 1:1–3. Admittedly, there are certain differences between the two stories. Most significant among them is the *Mechilta*'s suggestion (Parashat Bo 1) that Yonah's reticence to bring the gentile city of Nineveh to repent was based upon his concern that God would then compare the repentance of Nineveh to the lack of repentance among the Jews. Still, the differences fail to fully account for the difference in God's response.

is coerced to do exactly what God had ordered him to do in the first place.[19] Moshe, however, is not only allowed to reach a compromise, his obstinacy doesn't result in any punishment whatsoever. According to one opinion in the Talmud,[20] this represents a leniency that isn't afforded anyone else – being allowed to evoke Divine anger without being punished. The notion that Moshe could "get away" with his refusal to obey God is only underscored by its theologically problematic nature.

It may be helpful to examine Moshe's singular role in Jewish tradition to better understand God's response – or lack thereof – to his insubordination. After all, Moshe's leadership was truly exceptional, in both its scope and its grandeur: his mere proximity to God, as well as the enormity of taking the Jews out of Egypt and bringing them God's revelation, made his role unique. The power as well as the honor that would be accorded him would be the undoing of anyone with a less all-encompassing sense of humility. As the expression goes, "It's hard to be humble when you're great." Precisely for this reason, God was interested in a man whose natural humility was overwhelming, such that no matter what God said to him, he would still not see himself as someone fitting to speak on God's behalf. In other words, Moshe's humility was so fully integrated that the greatest arguments could not dissuade him from it. And for this reason, he was – shockingly – not even swayed by God.

Lest we think this absurd, we should bear in mind that certain things are so clear to us that we also would have trouble believing otherwise, even if God were to appear and tell us so. For example, if God were to tell us that we don't exist or that we don't breathe, would we really believe it? This was how Moshe saw the inappropriateness of his taking on the role that God requested of him. Moshe was asked to ignore his reservations and to accept that God always knows better, no matter how convinced he was of his perspective. Moshe clearly erred in his unwillingness to put aside his own worldview, which would make Divine anger completely justified. Be that as it may, however, the context

---

19 *Yonah* 3:14.

20 That of R. Yehoshua ben Karcha in *Zevachim* 102a. This view is opposed by R. Yosi, who maintains that Moshe is punished by having his progeny demoted from serving as priests in favor of Aharon's line.

made it a forgivable error, as – paradoxically – that is precisely what God was looking for in selecting this unique Jewish leader.

Though inappropriate, Moshe's tenacity was the only way that he could pass God's test. Moshe's refusal to listen to God showed to what extent he had internalized the requisite modesty his role demanded. It also showed that the place that would be given to him in the annals of human history would not cause him to lose his perspective. He would never lose sight of the fact that as a human being, no matter how great he would become, he would never fully and properly refract God's greatness.

◆ ◆ ◆

If uncertainty can itself be a sign of humility, there are some things that need to be clear to a person. It is a basic truth that a human being is very small. Both in how much physical space a person occupies and in how many years he lives, he is barely perceivable. The more objective one is, the more he can see this. Man's sole claim to importance has little to do with his intrinsic significance and everything to do with the fact that God chooses to relate to and to be concerned with him. Many great religious thinkers have tried to explain this Divine prerogative which, at the end of the day, will always be a nearly inexplicable kindness. Its mystery notwithstanding, ultimately, to use the words of Kohelet, "this is all of man."

Humility allows a person to understand his place in the grand scheme of things. Without such an understanding, a man is doomed to unduly focus on himself, and thus never become truly great. It is accordingly not accidental that the hallmark of Jewish holiness is humility.[21] Clearly, this is why Moshe, the most humble of all men, is the premier Jewish hero.

◆ ◆ ◆

Moshe makes us realize how central humility is to the fabric of Jewish values, but we mustn't stop there. It is incumbent upon us to fully incorporate that

---

21 Indeed, many great Jewish scholars have viewed humility as the most important virtue to acquire. See, for example, *Igeret haRamban*. Rambam also sees modesty as one of only two traits regarding which a person should not strive towards the golden mean but seek to take an extreme position (*Mishneh Torah*, Hilchot De'ot 2:3).

knowledge into contemporary Jewish life. Alas, this is not what we see in contemporary Western culture, which has often come to celebrate precisely those who are least humble. The American boxing champion, Mohammed Ali, who became beloved to many for constantly declaring, "I am the greatest," is only one example. Politicians, entertainers and other celebrities rise to success by flouting their real or imagined strengths. This is so pervasive that we are often not even aware of it or of how pernicious it is. In fact, the popularity of more than one contemporary Jewish leader is just as equally built around clever media exposure and other attention-getting maneuvers as any other celebrity.

In examining the acculturation of the Jewish people to Western society, it is particularly important to pick out which of its facets we should resist. Not only important for the preservation of our distinct identity, protesting the mistakes of the dominant culture is a great service to it as well, allowing it to put its own best foot forward. The centrality of human pride in Western culture, which has its roots in Enlightenment thinking and perhaps even earlier in Western culture's Greco-Roman pedigree, certainly demands our dissent.[22] Instead of protesting, however, Jews have more recently exaggerated their own sense of self-importance, both individually and nationally. Rather than protest, we are engaged in mimicry.

Living in an era dominated by publicity and fame, it is sometimes hard for us to realize that this is not the Jewish way. Yet even with all of the noise around us, we are obliged to listen to Moshe's stutter – a stutter far more eloquent than any speech or sonnet.

---

22 In fact, it is has been suggested that the exile brought about by Rome and its cultural descendants has been so long and bitter because the very core of this culture is the opposite of humility. See R. Eliyahu Dessler, *Michtav m'Eliyahu*, vol. 2, p. 51.

CHAPTER 3

Exile, Alienation and the Jewish Mission

> When a man is in his place, everyone knows him, and respects him according to his worth and according to the rank of his forbears. He, too, is familiar with his surroundings, knowing what he should say and what he should not say, what he should do and what he should not do. Once uprooted from his landscape, a man is at a loss, bewildered and perplexed. (Haim Sabato, *Aleppo Tales*)

IN THE LAST chapter, we explored the unusual self-awareness that Moshe brought into his first set of interviews with God. Of course, this perspective did not appear in a vacuum – as with everyone, Moshe was shaped by his life experience. In this chapter we will look at part of this experience, which will both resemble and yet be at variance with many other Biblical Jewish leaders.

Looking at Moshe's early life, we find a fascinating paradox: The greatest Jew to walk the face of the earth spent his childhood and youth in a completely non-Jewish culture. This forges the great irony that, as opposed to all the other Jews whom the Midrash praises for preserving their Jewish identities through keeping their Israelite names, language and dress,[1] young

*   I would like to thank my students, Eyal Cohen, Gila Fine, Elli Lifschitz, Ze'ev Orenstein, Dana Pulver, Jonathan Rossner and Adam Burnat, for their valuable input and suggestions on this essay, which they put forward in the context of an advanced seminar in which they were participants at the David Cardozo Academy, Jerusalem.

1   *Vayikra Rabba* 32:5. Though the extant versions of this midrash do not include

Moshe's name,[2] language and certainly mode of dress were all Egyptian.

Various commentators have noticed this and given explanations for the anomaly. Among them, the great nineteenth century commentator, Malbim,[3] writes that the royal court of Egypt was the best place for Moshe to acquire the characteristics and abilities that he would need to become the political and military leader of the Jewish people. This approach implies that had there been a Jewish monarch and court from which to learn, it would have been preferable for Moshe to avoid the court of Pharaoh. In other words, Moshe's apprenticeship in a foreign culture was due to the lack of a better option.

But there is another, more fundamental reason for Moshe's bicultural up-bringing, which sees Moshe's youth in a foreign court as a necessary part of his formation as the prime Jewish leader and recipient of the Torah. In order to fully appreciate this position, we will first want to compare Moshe's early life to the early life of one of his great predecessors.

Moshe's Exile and Ya'akov's Exile

There appear to be no two extended narratives in the entire Torah as similar as Ya'akov's exile to Lavan's house and Moshe's exile to Yitro's house.[4] The following narrative could uncannily describe either story:

After growing up in a privileged and sheltered environment, the hero runs away from a more powerful member of his household, who has made clear

---

clothing, various early commentators mention it, suggesting the existence of such a version.

2   See Ibn Ezra, R. Shmuel David Luzzatto, Malbim and R. Aryeh Kaplan (*Shemot* 2:10) on this point.

3   On *Shemot* 2:10.

4   See *Bereshit Rabba* 84:6, which suggests such an extended parallel between the lives of Ya'akov and *Yosef.* Nevertheless, a careful analysis of that comparison would show that many of the similarities are more coincidental. For example, the midrash tells us that both of their mothers had difficulty in childbirth, but in fact, the nature of these difficulties and their contexts are vastly different. (On some level, this and other differences create a "broken" analogy – one that is meant to set up a limited comparison as well as an important contrast.) The lives of young Ya'akov and Moshe, however, seem to parallel each other much more faithfully.

his intention to kill him. The hero goes east and ends up by a well, where his future wife faces an obstacle in watering her sheep. He removes the obstacle and waters the sheep for her. Quickly the shepherdess's father hears about this and takes in the hero, giving him his daughter as a wife and making him a shepherd over his flock. Eventually, after having children, he tells his father-in-law that he wants to return home. God speaks to the hero and he subsequently returns home to become leader of his clan. On the way back, he meets an otherworldly stranger who attacks him but ultimately relents. This is followed by a reunion with his older brother who markedly embraces him, in spite of the fact that the hero's return spells a threat to the older brother's position of leadership.

This astounding narrative analogy can be understood on two levels: (1) On the biographical level, we note the similarity between the *actual* events that transpired and (2) even more important, on the literary level, we note that the text *chooses to record* many of the parallel events, often in similar fashion. Since any biographical narrative will mention certain events and leave others out, when the Torah includes so many events that happen to both Ya'akov and Moshe, it is attempting to draw our attention to the similarities in the early lives of these two protagonists.

With parallel narratives, either one or both of them are highlighting the similarities in order to create a sort of internal commentary on the other (a literary technique referred to as intertextuality). This begs the question, "What are we supposed to gain by comparing the lives of Moshe and Ya'akov in their respective exiles?" Or to put it another way, why did Moshe's life not run as closely parallel to the lives of the other patriarchs, Avraham and Yitzchak?

One answer might be that Ya'akov and Moshe serve as the "bookends" of the exile in Egypt. As such, their lives are bound up with the concept of exile in a way that the lives of Avraham and Yitzchak are not. There is certainly much to say about this notion, but it fails to provide a comprehensive explanation to such a pronounced narrative analogy.

A more fundamental approach to the question may lie in the fact that both Ya'akov and Moshe are highly central characters. More specifically, both of them play out their lives at formative stages of the Jewish people's development.[5] Consequently, it appears that the type of seminal experiences that were common to Moshe and Ya'akov are a type of prerequisite in the life of a formative leader of the Jews.

The outstanding feature of the narrative analogy between Moshe and Ya'akov is their intense personal exile. They are in foreign lands, marry into (ultimately) foreign families, work with property that doesn't belong to them and live alongside unfamiliar cultural values.[6]

It is true that exile is not unique to these two great figures in the Jewish tradition. Avraham's very mission is born out of the command to go into exile. He is given the charge to move away from everything he knows in order to become a Jew. Not only that, even when he gets to the Promised Land, he soon feels impelled to move on to a new place of exile. It is also experienced – twice – by David. Yosef is sold into slavery and then taken into exile. Yehudah has his own version of exile when he temporarily leaves his family. The narrative of Yonah takes place almost exclusively in exile. In all of these cases, it is only when he is in exile that the Jewish hero comes into his own. This is hardly a coincidence. The central place of exile in what could be described as Jewish epic literature reveals it as a fundamental component in the heroic Jewish life.

5   Moshe's seminal influence on the Jewish nation goes without saying. It was he who took them out of Egyptian bondage to become a nation. It was also he who brought them to Mount Sinai to receive the Torah. If less obvious than in the case of Moshe, when we think carefully, a critical formative influence should be attributed to Ya'akov as well. Whereas the future of Avraham and Yitzchak's mission had been tenuous up until now, by the time Ya'akov transmitted that mission to the next generation, it lay on solid footing. If for no other reason, Ya'akov simply had many more offspring than either his father or his grandfather. Even more important, however, is the fact that he was able to put an end to the previous pattern, whereby only one child would take on the mission of his father. By having twelve sons who all accepted his vision and then transmitted it to their own children, Ya'akov created the demographic basis for the Jewish people. In this way, his efforts to create the physical basis of the Jewish people parallel Moshe's efforts to form the ideological basis of the nation later on.

6   This is most powerfully driven home by Lavan, who tells Ya'akov that he couldn't have given him his younger daughter before his older daughter because "such is not the practice in *our* place." Whether Lavan is lying or not, Ya'akov seems to accept the basis of the argument, showing agreement that Ya'akov is, in fact, not completely familiar with the ethics of his host culture.

Still, the intensity of exile experienced by Moshe and Ya'akov makes their lives the most intimately and meaningfully connected with this experience. Having identified the key variable in the life of a formative Jewish leader, we now need to analyze its significance.

Exile and Alienation

In the best of circumstances, exile automatically breeds some level of personal alienation. The man in exile initially experiences estrangement from the new host culture to which he is transplanted. The new nation does things in ways that appear strange and unnatural to him. Eventually, however, he begins to feel alienated from his own ancestral culture as well. The strangeness of the new culture starts to dissipate as he experiences their ways on a more regular basis. In fact, depending on the amount and proximity of exposure he or his children have to the new host culture, it is now the "old ways" of his ancestral culture which start to seem unnatural. If familiarity to the new culture facilitates its adoption, so do the benefits frequently bestowed by the host culture onto its new adherents. To give an example from American Jewish history, one of the main causes for Jewish immigrants' estrangement from Judaism was the tangible rewards earned by those who adapted to American culture. If this was occasionally lost on the first generation of immigrants, it rarely escaped the attention of the second and third generations. As a result of this conditional advancement, many a Jew felt prompted to take a more critical view of the ancestral institutions of Shabbat, kashrut and the like – often impediments to upward mobility – allowing them to more easily justify abandoning these practices.

Even beyond assimilatory behavior, estrangement from a comfortable collective identity brings doubt about one's very identity. If, for example, one is a Jewish-American, one automatically has a hyphenated identity. A question that such a person will have to face is, "Am I more Jewish or more American?" Moreover, if we are speaking about a person's cultural identity, can he really be both Jewish *and* American? Or is culture not an exclusive affair, such that one who attempts to be bicultural ends up being neither really American nor really Jewish? Here too we can look at Jewish-American literature, with its characteristic angst. Through their protagonists, authors of this genre are often grappling with their own evolving bicultural identities and consequent alienation.

Although rare is the man who actually chooses exile, the resultant detachment from a clear and obvious path is not without its benefits. Exile prompts one to greater independence in value formation and, subsequently, in decision making. He has at least two options open to him – to act according to the values of his own ancestral culture or according to the values of his new host culture. Since most people do things because "it's simply what's done," once a person is confronted with the fact that two different groups with which he identifies do things differently, he must make a thoughtful choice about which approach he will adopt. And once the automatic monopoly on what to do is broken, it suggests that other choices are out there as well. A person who needs to think about his course of action will often be led to consider other possibilities that he previously did not realize existed. Simply put, *once two choices are available, nearly all choices become available.*

Indeed, in many respects, this is the situation of modern man. Though there are still many things that we do simply because "that's what's done," there are many areas in which living in a culturally cosmopolitan world has made us aware of our choices (often to the point of paralysis!).

Hence it could be said that Ya'akov's and Moshe's exiles made them into proto-modern men. Moreover, if our modern personal state of autonomy is, indeed, largely a result of our lack of cultural roots, then the more uprooted a person, the more autonomous we can expect him to be. In that case, the extreme nature of Ya'akov's and Moshe's exiles likely led them to a heightened level of deliberation and thoughtfulness, such as would rarely be found in even the most modern of men.

Having briefly considered the effects of exile on a person, we are now in a better position to understand why Ya'akov and Moshe had to endure such an intense version of this experience. It appears that the Torah is interested in specifically *these* great leaders' making their own decisions. For this to happen, the alienation of exile would first need to facilitate transcendence of the values which they might otherwise have automatically shared with their ancestral and/or host cultures.

It is not that Ya'akov and Moshe would be free of human terms and concepts. One could not expect that from any person.[7] Rather, they would be enriched by the multiplicity of human approaches to which they were exposed and would as a result become unusually thought*ful* leaders. And, as we will discuss later, it is this thoughtfulness that would bolster the Jewish tradition's unusual cultural transcendence and accompanying universal appeal.

Moshe the Outsider

Having seen the centrality of exile and loneliness for the formative Jewish leader, we can still ask whether this solitude need be absolute or whether such a leader can still have some attachments nonetheless. The answer to that question may depend on a further distinction that will lead to different answers for Ya'akov and Moshe.

The characteristic existential loneliness that we described in the previous section is felt in the best of exiles. In the case of Ya'akov and Moshe, however, it is compounded by the additional hardship of having to go it alone. If someone has to undergo exile, he would almost always prefer to be accompanied by his family and, if possible, even by his community.[8] Similarly, once in exile this man commonly marries within his own ancestral community so as to ease the

---

7   There is a growing literature on the centrality of a person's culture to his way of looking at the world and his resulting values. In the footsteps of Alisdair MacIntyre's *After Virtue* (especially Chapter 10), communitarianism and multiculturalism have stressed the implausibility of some sort of abstract "man" in a cultural vacuum as had been implicitly assumed in classical liberalism. The leading representatives of communitarianism are Michael Sandel – see *Liberalism and the Limits of Justice* (Cambridge: Cambridge University Press, 1982) and *Democracy's Discontent* (Cambridge, MA: Harvard University Press, 1996), and Amitai Etzioni – see *New Communitarian Thinking* (Charlottesville: University Press of Virginia, 1995). The leading representative of multiculturalism is Will Kymlicka – see *Multicultural Citizenship* (Oxford: Clarendon Press, 1995) and most recently *Politics in the Vernacular* (Oxford: Oxford University Press, 2001). See also the important emendation to Kymlicka's thought by Avishai Margalit and Moshe Halbertal in "Liberalism and the Right to Culture" (*Social Research* 61:3; Fall 1994).

8   See Rashi on *Vayikra* 26:33 based on *Sifra*, Parashat Bechukotai 6:6. Accordingly, the

effects of alienation, at least within the four walls of his own home. In contrast to this, Ya'akov and Moshe arrive all alone. Having no other realistic choice, they marry cross-culturally and father children who grow up in the culture of their wives. True, it is Ya'akov's parents who tell him it is better that he marry specifically in exile. Still, this does not make his ordeal much easier. In both cases, it is likely that some of the difficulties that these two great men experience in their marriages stem from the increased complexity engendered when a man in exile enters a cross-cultural marriage.

Be that as it may, Moshe's loneliness is not exactly the same as Ya'akov's. Since Ya'akov had certain advantages in this regard, he is able to create bonds with his foreign wives that Moshe is not. One such advantage is that he is able to marry his cousins, even if he didn't know them until he moved out of his home. Moreover, his exile was to a land that his grandfather Avraham could still refer to as "his land and his birthplace."[9] Granted, it is neither Ya'akov's land nor his birthplace, but neither was it completely foreign. In contrast, when Moshe goes to Midian, it is to an altogether foreign place and foreign family. Yet even after taking all these differences into account, Moshe's highly unusual relationship with his wife and children needs further analysis.

The Complete Alienation of Moshe

Though there are, in fact, several major differences in the two narratives under discussion,[10] when it comes to the issue of alienation, the interaction presented between Ya'akov and his wives on the one hand and Moshe and his wife, Tzipporah, on the other, takes on far more importance than anything else. Compared with the description of the marriages of Ya'akov and his wives, the story of Moshe and Tzipporah is highly truncated. In fact, Tzipporah's name appears only three times in the entire Torah. What we do hear about

---

"exile" of an accidental killer is softened by the stipulation that he be accompanied by his teacher or students into a city of refuge (*Makkot* 10a).

9 *Bereshit* 24:4, 7.

10 A contrast worthy of study but not obviously relevant to the present discussion is the difference in the relationship between Ya'akov and Moshe and their respective fathers-in-law. We will look at this contrast more carefully in Chapter 5.

the relationship between Moshe and his spouse leads us to conclude that it was emotionally distant. Even before their final separation alluded to in the book of *Bemidbar*,[11] Moshe and Tzipporah had already known a protracted geographical separation, something unknown to any other couple in the entire Torah.[12] This early separation would not only impact on the frequency of their interaction, it would also set its tone.

Indeed, Tzipporah remains largely invisible. To begin with, she is almost entirely silent – we hear her voice only briefly, when she appears to give Moshe some sort of rebuke concerning the circumcision of their son.[13] Otherwise, we don't hear from her at all.

Related to the paucity of interaction between Moshe and his wife is the parallel lack of connection between Moshe and his children, who at one point are appropriately referred to as "the children of Tzipporah."[14] The Torah tells us almost nothing about Moshe's children – even less, in fact, than it tells us about Tzipporah. That being the case, we are almost surprised when the Torah uncharacteristically focuses even briefly on the significance of their names.[15] This is all in marked contrast to the detailed and colorful description of Ya'akov and his children.

Moreover, the anomaly here is not just terseness; the curious fragmentation also demands our attention. This is seen most clearly in the middle of the

---

11 12:1–4.

12 See *Shemot* 18:2.

13 Though even this is far from clear. Some suggest that Tzipporah is not addressing Moshe at all, but rather their son. (See, for example, Rashi on *Shemot* 4:25, presumably based on the comments of Rabban Shimon ben Gamliel in *Nedarim* 32b.)

14 *Shemot* 18:2 (see Netziv) and especially 18:6, where Yitro refers to himself as Moshe's father-in-law, to Tzipporah as Moshe's wife, but to Gershom and Eliezer as *Tzipporah's* children. Though the narrative seems to describe them as "his" (i.e., Moshe's) sons in 18:5, the reference is not entirely clear and "his" could be referring to Yitro and not to Moshe (see *Perush Yonatan* on *Targum Yonatan*, which mentions this possibility). The one clear reference to them as Moshe's children appears in *Shemot* 4:20, when Moshe has not yet returned to Egypt to focus on his mission. In other words, they may have begun as his children but they soon enough become his wife's children.

15 *Shemot* 18:3–4.

journey back to Egypt, when a second, unnamed child suddenly appears.[16] Neither introduced nor explained, his very name is revealed to us only later. In another place, the Torah tells us that Tzipporah came back to see Moshe "after he had sent her away"[17] – as if we already knew this. In fact, it comes totally out of the blue: Earlier, the text tells us only that Moshe's family started on the road back to Egypt with him. From that point onward, his family is no longer mentioned, making us assume that they had been with him the entire time. After all, we don't hear anything that would make us believe otherwise, and the default of Biblical couples is to stay together.

One could perhaps suggest that the difference between the Torah's interest in Ya'akov's family and its lack of interest in Moshe's is due to a greater need for the mothers' influence on the formative stages of the Jewish people. And because the children of Ya'akov *were* the Jewish people at that time, it makes sense that the Torah would focus on them. In contrast, by the time Moshe appeared on the scene, the Jewish people were a large nation, which made Moshe's wife and two sons were much less central to the further development of Jewish history.

Along these lines, it is possible to argue that Moshe's children didn't *do* anything that would warrant their inclusion in the text. No doubt all of this is true. Still, the Torah's terse and fragmented presentation of Tzipporah and her children seems too extreme to be completely accounted for by these explanations. Consequently, it would make much more sense to say that the main reason for this extraordinary presentation has more to do with Moshe himself than it has to do with any external factors.

To help us understand Moshe's unique isolation, we should turn briefly to the relationship between Ya'akov and his wives. Though we see a similar alienation from his general surroundings, his relationship at least with Rachel can hardly be described as distant. Nor should the dichotomy between his isolation from others on the one hand and the emotional closeness with this wife on the other come as a surprise. It may well be the very intensity of his separation that pushes him closer to Rachel. The loneliest of men can find a

---

16 Ibid., 4:20.
17 Ibid., 18:2. See Rashbam for an alternative explanation.

welcome vestige of existential communion in the relationship with his wife.[18] This allows a person to find the strength to endure isolation from others when such separation is necessary.

But Moshe was destined for a different fate. It appears that the one who would receive the Torah could not be entirely "human." The demanded level of uninterrupted spirituality would require someone as removed from the human condition as possible. Close involvement with someone else, no matter how spiritually uplifting, would necessarily come at the expense of some of his direct involvement with God.[19] The same would be true of Moshe's role as a father. Being involved with his children would also have come at the cost of the intensity of his relationship with God.[20]

Indeed, the angels' objection to Moshe's receiving the Torah is couched in the phrase that he was "born of a woman."[21] Their complaint could be understood as pointing to Moshe's intrinsic inability to escape his human bias.[22] We can choose to have no intimate human bonds – except for the bond with the person who bore us. For the angels, that unavoidable human bond disqualified Moshe from being the bearer of the superhuman document called the Torah. This observation notwithstanding, Moshe does separate himself from others as much as is *humanly* possible.

18 It is well-known that Rav Yosef Dov Soloveitchik, the author of the somewhat autobiographical *The Lonely Man of Faith*, found great solace in the companionship of his wife.

19 One may then raise the question of why Moshe should have gotten married at all. I can think of two approaches to this problem. On a very basic level, a person has to *develop* into greatness. This means that the Moshe who married Tzipporah was not the same Moshe who would later separate from her. But there is perhaps another, more important answer. Marriage is an important part of human life and a person who does not know it from the inside cannot properly lead other people in living their lives. Even if celibacy allows a person to focus more on the spiritual (as with the Talmud's Ben Azzai), it still prevents him from a deeper understanding of this central part of human existence. Though the receiver of the Torah could not be totally human, the first teacher of the Torah could not be anything but completely human. While Moshe had to be as removed as any human being would ever be, he simultaneously had to be personally familiar with what human life is about.

20 See *Redeeming Relevance in Genesis*, Chapter 2.

21 *Shabbat* 88b.

22 See Chapter 2, p. 40, for a related discussion of this midrash.

This is not true of Ya'akov, who actually spends a great deal of energy on family matters. Inasmuch as Ya'akov represents the earlier stage of proto-nation building, his alienation need not be as complete as Moshe's, as it is the latter who builds the true foundations of the Jewish people. In this sense, Ya'akov is in point of fact an earlier, yet necessarily incomplete, prototype of Moshe. He sets up the mode of behavior in order for it to be perfected by Moshe later on. When it was time for Moshe to take on his role, however, his alienation would need to be total. Even the last stronghold of human bonding and communion that we find in marriage would have been counterproductive for his particular mission. In this sense, Moshe can be described as the most, and maybe the only truly, lonely man of faith. But what type of faith is generated by this type of complete alienation from others?

Moshe the Universal Leader

We know that the human bonds to community and family are a great blessing. But as with anything else, it is a blessing that comes at a cost. On the one hand, family and community are just about essential to the creation of identity and, ultimately, of meaning.[23] But these same bonds of loyalty that allow us to be more receptive and helpful to our own group are also what prevent us from being more understanding of those outside our circle. We all understand events from the perspective of a specific community; this is the way we make sense of our experiences. In turn, this prevents us from seeing events in the same way as they are seen by others. It is humanly impossible to give complete and total support to two competing narratives of the same story.

Moshe's alienation from his wife, his family and his nation allowed him to transcend the normal boundaries that separate us from those outside these circles. He *could* not remain tied to his family. Otherwise, there would always be an in-group and a resultant out-group. This is what made Moshe into a universal leader – he could identify with other groups as easily as he could identify with his family; with non-Jews as easily as with Jews. As a result, when

23 See note 7, above.

considering Moshe, other nations would not perceive an unfriendly bias that would disqualify him from their allegiance.

The rabbinic tradition that Moshe insisted on bringing the group of foreigners known as *eiruv rav* (the mixed multitude) out of Egypt along with the native-born Jews[24] serves to strengthen our contention. Moreover, it leads to the conclusion that Moshe's experience with other cultures does not end when he comes back "home" to his own people. Moshe remains a leader of mankind even when he becomes the leader of the Jews.

Moshe's stance may well be grounded in the nature of the Torah itself: While sometimes overlooked, the Jewish understanding of revelation is far from being an exclusively Jewish affair. The Torah describes the Jews as a nation of priests,[25] meaning that they have a responsibility to spread the Torah's moral and religious principles beyond the Jewish people. How they are to do that is beyond the scope of the current discussion, but it is clear that this is a major goal of the Jewish people. To put it differently, even as the Torah's specific laws are meant for the Jews, its ethical and spiritual vision is intended for all of mankind. Thus, the Torah has an uncommon dual identity, addressing a specific national culture on the one hand yet implicitly speaking to all who are created in the image of God on the other.

As the central figure and communicator of this dual doctrine, Moshe needed a dual identity: to be a representative of the Jewish people and still also be a true citizen of the world. Only in this way would Moshe be able to receive the Torah in both of its dimensions. As such, the faith of Moshe is the faith of man as man as well as that of man as Jew.[26]

---

24 See *Shemot Rabba* 42:6.
25 *Shemot* 19:6.
26 Parallel to his dual identity is Moshe's need for domestic bifurcation. He must be the completely objective leader of the Jewish nation as if he didn't have a family, and yet he needed to be grounded in an actual family framework to allow him to relate to normative human experience.

Moshe the Jew

Moshe's alienation did not only benefit the world at large, it also brought significant direct benefits for the Jewish people as well. Moshe was in charge of leading the Jews through the greatest revolution in history – a revolution that would require them to address their faults in as complete a fashion as possible. Such leadership could only come from someone who saw the Jews objectively – who could recognize their weaknesses unapologetically. As mentioned earlier, it is a natural tendency for a person to assume the values of his culture, even when these values are not ideal. From this point of view, there was a need for the Jews to be led by an "outsider."[27]

At the same time, being purely objective is not what was desired of Moshe either. Cold objectivity makes it more difficult to feel the nation's suffering – and easier to say that *they* deserve these punishments. Although Moshe's foreign objectivity benefited the Jewish people, he could not be their leader if he did not empathize with their affliction. So even though Moshe had to be raised by Egyptians, his earliest childhood had to be among Jews. He had to be emotionally connected from the crib. This early connection was needed to connect an ultimately universal Torah with the specific nation that was destined to fulfill it. Indeed, as a leader, Moshe needed to have both of these qualifications – objective universal intellect and subjective Jewish emotion.

Exile and the Jews

Returning to Moshe's universal role, it is not only the Torah of Moshe that has a universal side to it, it appears that the Jewish people itself has a universal

---

27 It is in this spirit too, that *Tosefot Yeshanim* understands the statement in the Talmud that "converts are like a scab to the Jewish people" (*Yevamot* 47b). This Talmudic commentary implies that the convert does not have any role models and thus performs the mitzvot the way they are *supposed* to be performed and not necessarily the way they are *actually* performed. As such, his unusually model conduct is abrasive to the rest of the Jews, who are used to a lower standard since "this is simply the way things are done."

side as well. More than any other nation, the Jews are called upon to perform a transnational function.

Hence, it could well be that the cultural alienation experienced most powerfully by our formative leaders is something that the Jewish people would need to experience on a national level as well. As Moshe would have to be a universal man, the Jews too would have to be a universal nation. From this perspective, it should come as no surprise that the Jewish people has known more years of exile than of statehood.

The Jews' relationship to exile is based not only on its being the more frequent situation in which they have found themselves. Exile is also a key element in the very foundation of the Jewish people. The Torah makes a point of telling us that Avraham was not born or raised in Israel.[28] Just as he was born outside his homeland, the Jewish nation too would have to be "born" outside their homeland (i.e., in Egypt). This means that the Jew's relationship to his land is not the same as that of other nations. He belongs in it but he also belongs out of it.[29]

And whether it was God's original intention or not, the so-called "wandering Jew" is an almost ubiquitous feature of our world. The Jews are a nation that maintains its own identity in exile even as it assumes much of the cultural trappings of its hosts. Indeed, Jews don't only resemble their gentile neighbors, they often take a leading role in their societies. A Jew is both a Jew and a universal man. This unique situation is perhaps the result of being the spokesperson for a document that is meant as much for universal consumption as it is for Jewish consumption.

Beyond Avraham's foreshadowing our identity as strangers, we also see that this very first Jew created a tone of concern for others outside his immediate sphere. He did this by praying for wicked neighboring communities, taking care of wandering strangers and rebuking leaders who did not live up to their moral calling. By embedding these actions into its first stories, the Torah forever binds the Jew to all those with whom he comes into contact. From these

---

28 *Bereshit* 11:26–31.

29 This consciousness could be one of the main functions of the sabbatical year, wherein a Jew temporarily relinquishes ownership of his agricultural land.

beginnings, the Torah develops this theme more fully in the uniquely transcendent personality of Moshe.

◆ ◆ ◆

The Jew is called to emulate Moshe and somehow try to hear the national
narratives of others – to be above his own culture while he lives within it.
In the post-nationalist world of today, the Jewish take on nationalism is extremely useful. For in truth, contemporary post-nationalism is only one side
of today's equation. Although increasingly permeable national borders result
in their taking on less importance, nationalism is still not entirely a thing of
the past. Nor is it likely (or even desirable) that it will completely disappear
in the foreseeable future. The problem raised by the vestiges of nationalism
in an increasingly multicultural global community is how to simultaneously
cling to the meaning given by one's own particular identity and still be able
to work with others who don't share it. Hence, the unique Jewish model just
explained could make a singular contribution. Properly understood, Jewish
duality represents the notion of a people comfortable with its own tradition
yet sufficiently alienated from it to listen to competing narratives. Such a paradigm allows for the grounding influence of one's own culture while leaving
room for other visions of the good.

Alienation from Above

If we have begun to understand the reasons for Moshe's exile, we have certainly
not exhausted the topic. It may prove useful to revisit the fact that Moshe (as
well as Ya'akov) spent most of his days in exile as a shepherd. The motif of a
young Jewish leader as a shepherd or shepherdess is actually found in several
places.[30] The leading of sheep is meant to prepare and foreshadow a future
leader's responsibility for his "flock," the Jewish people.[31] Nonetheless, when

---

30 See especially Kli Yakar (also R. Bachya and Netziv) on *Shemot* 3:1 on why so many
    Jewish prophets (and leaders) had been shepherds in their youth.
31 See Abarbanel on *Shemot* 3:1.

we look at Moshe and Ya'akov, here too we see that they deviate somewhat from the standard version of this motif.

In the standard shepherd scenario, the sheep are obviously analogous to the Jewish people.[32] More subtle is the further analogy created by the fact that the shepherd-leader is usually tending his or her *father's* flock.[33] The father, of course, represents God.[34] Thus, the full imagery is of the Jewish people as God's flock, which He entrusts to faithful caretakers. If we look more carefully, an ordinary shepherd has two primary responsibilities – to protect his sheep from predators and to make sure that they find food to eat and water to drink. This is exactly the two main responsibilities of the Jewish leader: to protect them from their enemies and to provide them with sustenance, both physical and spiritual.[35]

In the cases of Moshe and Ya'akov, the analogy is more nuanced. While the master still represents God and the sheep continue to represent the Jewish people, the relationship of shepherd to both flock and master is different from the classical case where the leader tends his father's sheep. Ya'akov and Moshe were watching sheep that did not belong to them.[36] They were essentially tending a *foreign flock* for a *foreign master*.

Hence, when Ya'akov and Moshe would become the shepherds of the Jewish people, they would not relate to the sheep as their own, and more important, they would not relate to the owner of the sheep as their Father. If we may at first doubt such a conclusion, when we look at the relationship of

---

32 The Jewish nation is compared to a flock and its rulers referred to as shepherds more than once in the Bible itself – see for example, *Bemidbar* 27:17, where Moshe asks for a worthy successor that will prevent the Jews from being "like a flock without a shepherd" and *Tehillim* 77:21, where Moshe and Aharon are described as the shepherds of the Jewish people.

33 Such as David and the sons of Ya'akov (and maybe Rachel and Tzipporah). If we expand this category to include herdsmen, we can also add Amos, Elisha and Shaul.

34 The comparison is most familiar to us from the Jewish liturgy, especially from the *Avinu, Malkenu* (Our Father, our King) prayer. Nonetheless, this imagery can already be found in the Bible – see, for example, *Yirmeyahu* 31:8.

35 The well-known comparison of Torah to water only reinforces the significance of the shepherd analogy.

36 See Malbim on *Shemot* 3:2, who makes this observation concerning Moshe.

these two great men with the Jewish people and with God, we truly see that there is a greater degree of separation than we might expect.

For example, when Moshe sees the negative effect his mission is having on the Jewish people, he laments to God about the state of "this people" and "Your people," but not "*my* people."[37] Moreover, God's possibly rhetorical suggestion to Moshe that He would destroy the Jewish people and create a new nation from Moshe[38] only adds to the notion that Moshe represents a shepherd who is not completely identified with his flock. Moshe's unique stance is further seen from his many arguments with both the Jewish people and with God, acting once on this side and once on the other, as we would expect from an independent third party.

Granted, this distinction of the shepherd as separate from God and from the Jewish people is less clear when it comes to Ya'akov. Though Ya'akov is not as passive as his father Yitzchak, neither does he appear to be as independent as his grandfather Avraham. However, his wrestling with what tradition describes as an angel[39] is unprecedented and certainly bespeaks independence – far beyond the autonomy typified by the arguments that Avraham had with God. Since an angel is an agent of God, standing up against it is a type of insubordination, if apparently an acceptable one. From this incident alone it would seem that Ya'akov is not as pliant as we might otherwise think. A further indication of his independent attitude is his removal of the God-given birthright from Reuven. A careful reading of the Ya'akov narrative shows us a determined patriarch who, if not as dramatic as Moshe, is still capable of disagreeing with his Master as well as with his flock.

In short, the position of Ya'akov and Moshe toward their flock is that of a manager whose job it is to detachedly determine both the master's and the sheep's best interests, not necessarily his own. His interests and theirs are not

---

37 *Shemot* 5:22–23. This parallels perfectly Moshe's relationship with the actual sheep that he had once tended for his father-in-law. There too, he could have referred to the sheep as these sheep or your (Yitro's) sheep but not as my (Moshe's) sheep.

38 Ibid., 32:10. The discussion that precedes and ensues God's suggestion is also worthy of note, in that God first calls the Jews *Moshe's* nation, to which Moshe responds by calling them *God's* nation.

39 *Bereshit Rabba* 77:3.

always identical, as he is not self-employed or working for blood relatives. For those who are, financial security is completely tied to the outcome of their work, for it is their own property that they aim to preserve and increase.

The relationship of a manager to both the master and the flock is obviously more removed and less emotional than that of a shepherd toward his or his own father's flock. In this regard, it is sometimes easier to manage someone else's money than one's own, since the emotional concerns that can lead to bad business decisions are avoided. A manager is typically less afraid to take a calculated risk since he doesn't identify with the possible loss as intensely as if it were his own money.

Yet the detachment of Ya'akov and Moshe from the Master and His flock may well have importance beyond its contribution to their effectiveness. As mentioned, an employee formulates his interests separately from his employer. Even when the employer was God, the Torah wants us to note the autonomy of the managers. In this context, we should remember the highly symbolic wrestling of Ya'akov[40] and note that a similarly symbolic scene is reenacted on some level when Moshe and his wife meet their otherworldly assailant on their way to Egypt.[41]

In thinking about a religious leader – and certainly a prophet – we would naturally assume that he needs to draw himself as close to God as possible. In this regard, it is surprising to see that Moshe assumes a certain distance from God. Exactly because it is surprising, it is also instructive.

It is axiomatic that God wants man to obey Him and to elect to do His will. But He also wants a genuine partnership. That is to say, He wants a man to be a free agent who comes to agree with God neither from meek submission nor from cultural tradition. Precisely because both Moshe and Ya'akov would become so close to God, He had to make sure that they would perceive God's interests (as well as those of the Jewish people) separately from their own. This is especially true concerning Moshe: the man who would become God's humble servant is most clearly in danger of losing his own independent perspective. Moshe's separation from his wife and temporary abstinence from

40 *Bereshit* 32:25–31.
41 *Shemot* 4:24–26.

food and drink[42] only underscore the danger of his losing his humanity – i.e., that which makes him a genuine partner of God.

In the case of Moshe, it was necessary for the man who would receive and first teach the Torah to lay the groundwork for the partnership between man and God that Jews would subsequently call *Talmud Torah*. This is maybe best summarized through the classic rabbinic dictum, "*lo beshamayim hee*" (the Torah is not in Heaven). Via this principle, the Jewish people has enshrined the idea that God wants man – within certain parameters – to decide for himself the best way to understand the Torah.

◆ ◆ ◆

In the final analysis, the Jewish tradition's unusual involvement with exile and alienation is precisely that which makes it particularly Jewish. Ironically, those very elements that we identify as "Jewish" also give Judaism its relevance to mankind as a whole. Without putting the importance of nation completely aside, the Torah teaches all men to recognize the centrality of universal human values. Connectedly, the narratives we have studied also illustrate God's insistence that man be human and not superhuman – to accept the legitimacy of his own emotions, needs and aspirations in order to formulate that which is incumbent upon him to request from his Almighty Partner.

Perhaps the following midrash most succinctly illustrates how Moshe combined a universalist ethic with human autonomy:

> [The mixed multitude is called Moshe's] people. Moshe said, "Master of the world, what is the reason that they are my people?" God said to him, "They are your people because when they were still in Egypt . . . I told you not to mix them in with the [native-born] Jews and *since you were humble and righteous* you told me, One should always take penitents. And since I knew what they would do I said no, but *I [still] did as you wanted.*"[43]

42 Ibid., 34:28. (See also Rambam in *Mishneh Torah*, Hilchot Yesodei Hatorah 7:6.)
43 *Shemot Rabba* 42:6 (emphasis mine).

After the mixed multitude is identified as the group who worshiped the golden calf, Moshe is castigated for his lack of proper judgment. Still, the midrash approves of Moshe's motivation to the point that it tells us that God accepted his argument. In doing so, the midrash reiterates the monumental significance of his stance – a stance born of exile and alienation.

◆ ◆ ◆

The return of Jewish statehood has brought many challenges with it. Even as the opportunities created are myriad, one of its greatest spiritual challenges is the resultant effacement of our sense of exile. As we see from our great formative leaders, this is part of our national legacy and thus its loss is not completely positive – at least, not unless we can continue to dip into the consciousness of our historical alienation and transculturalism and make it a cardinal feature of the still-new Jewish state.

In this context, it is interesting to speculate that the development of the State of Israel has roughly coincided with another phenomenon that could help to remedy the isolationist trends that come naturally with statehood. The so-called *ba'al teshuva* community (returnees to traditional Judaism), from which I draw my own roots and with which I still have much contact, is the segment of committed Jewry that grew up in the "Egyptian court." This means that they have the ability to be more objective about the Jewish people and constructively point out its weaknesses. By and large, this is not what we see. Instead, the more objective viewpoint of the *ba'al teshuva* is often criticized as foreign, causing most returnees to question their own frequently legitimate perspective and to bow to the pressures of traditional society.

I remember discussing a certain series of children's books with a kindergarten teacher working for me at an Israeli school a few years back. I told her that I did not feel the books were appropriate, as all the non-Jewish characters were caricatured as stupid and anti-semitic. She responded by saying that she did not understand what I meant and that I had a somewhat "goyish" view of things. My thought was that my point of view was in fact much more "Jewish" than hers – I wonder if Moshe's leadership was also castigated for being "goyish"?

When I was criticized by my employee, I had two advantages that most *ba'alei teshuva* do not have. First, I was her supervisor and, "goyish" or not, I was the one who made the final decision. Secondly, I had pursued my Torah studies to the point where I could feel self-confident in my own understanding of Jewish tradition.

Be that as it may, all *ba'alei teshuva* need to realize that veteran religious Jews are not always correct in their opinions, and base much more than they might think on "this is simply how things are done." Much of the *ba'al teshuva's* initial dissatisfaction with his new world comes from a greater objectivity. And just as objectivity was needed in the time of Moshe to help the Jews improve themselves, so too is it needed today if the Jews are to truly improve themselves. Coming to this realization is not just good for the *ba'al teshuva*, it is, more important, good for the Jewish people as a whole.

CHAPTER 4

Two Brothers and a Sister: The Family Team

The theme of sibling relationships first appears near the very beginning of the Torah. There, the relationship of the world's first two brothers, Kayin and Hevel, could well be described as nothing less than a disaster. Things improve only slightly as we move on to Yitzchak and Yishmael, then to Ya'akov and Esav, Leah and Rachel and finally to the thirteen children of Ya'akov. In all of these stories, rivalry and jealousy are central forces at play.[1]

While each of the first four scenarios mentioned above consists of only one sibling versus the other,[2] the number of Ya'akov's children complicates that story's direct comparison to the others. But that narrative is more complex for other reasons as well. We now have many children, at least three of whom are vying for leadership.[3] Moreover, these competitors are distinguished by being from different, yet ostensibly equal, mothers. In spite of these differences, however, the general theme is very similar: The competition for dominance leads to a situation where one of the brothers needs to be somehow eliminated – via either banishment or murder. In the case of Kayin and Hevel, the latter's elimination is accomplished by murder. In the case of Yitzchak and

---

1   We have admittedly skipped over mention of Shem, Cham and Yefet who, at least at one point, work in partnership. We have done so taking our cue from the Biblical text, which give us little detail about their relationship.
2   Avraham's younger sons from Ketura seem to be in a different category and so, for all practical purposes, don't really figure in to the rivalry that we find between Yitzchak and Yishmael.
3   I.e., Reuven, Yehudah and Yosef. See *Redeeming Relevance in Genesis*, Chapter 6.

Yishmael, Yishmael is eliminated by banishment. In the next story, it is the hero, Ya'akov, who gets banished in order to avoid being murdered. In similar fashion, Yosef's brothers need to choose between the two options available, first preferring murder and subsequently reversing their decision in favor of banishment.[4]

In the Beginning, There Was a Problem

The problem that plagues one generation after another throughout the book of *Bereshit* is a major key in the development of mankind, namely, How does one cooperate with another human being outside of the nuclear family? (By nuclear family, I mean one's spouse and children.)

Though the Biblical extended family may have been much more bound together than its modern counterpart, the Torah shows that any extended family is intrinsically disunified. The very existence of several nuclear families creates a zero-sum game, most powerfully manifested when it comes to the sharing of inheritance. This is dovetailed on a more global scale by the finite nature of goods available in the world at large. The latter is illustrated by a midrash about the fight between the first two brothers, wherein Kayin and Hevel divvy up the world, with one getting all the real estate whereas the other would get everything else. The former demanded that his brother not set foot on the entire world since it all belonged to him, and the latter demanded that the other surrender any clothing that he would want to wear since these all belonged to him.[5] The implicit irony of this midrash is produced by the finite limits of what can be possessed. If someone else possesses something, the only way for me to possess it is to somehow take it from him. As a result, and as in the case of Kayin and Hevel, if I want or need that item badly enough, it may not end nicely.

But the difficulty of brotherly cooperation goes beyond material goods.

---

4   It is interesting to note that this motif doesn't get fully played out in the competition between Rachel and Leah, which can perhaps be more accurately viewed as following the conventions of another familiar motif – that of rival wives (e.g. Sarah and Hagar, Peninah and Chanah, etc.).
5   *Bereshit Rabba* 22:7.

The institution of *yibum* (levirate marriage) and the resistance shown to it in its first appearance, when Yehudah's sons were expected to perform it, is a good example of the natural resistance to cooperation within the extended family and especially among brothers.[6] Here too, the concept of zero-sum rears its problematic head. Even in this less tangible realm, it is unnatural to want to give something to someone else if by doing so, one is divesting himself of that same thing.

Lest we think this is limited to the male gender, the rivalry between Rachel and Leah is hardly less intense, turning sour when Leah accuses Rachel of stealing her husband.[7] A husband married to more than one woman is also a zero-sum situation and Leah knows that when Rachel is able to grab Ya'akov's attention, it will likely come at the cost of time and attention – and perhaps even children – that he might otherwise have given her.

Difficult as it may be, creating a paradigm of cooperation beyond the nuclear family has tremendous ramifications in the building of a smoothly functioning society. Anticipating this issue, the Bible shows us long before Hobbes that without cooperation between different households, life would indeed be "nasty, brutish and short."

The Paradigm Shift

When we eventually come to Moshe and his siblings, the motif of sibling interaction undergoes a radical transformation. The implicit competition for leadership that perforce exists between Moshe and his siblings does not turn into a quest for Moshe's elimination. On the contrary, Miriam makes sure that he doesn't die in infancy and Aharon goes looking for him to accompany him back from his exile.

Indeed, the Torah not only highlights the cooperation of these three siblings, it refers to them as brother, brother and sister with unusual frequency and in pointedly unusual ways. For example, Miriam first comes onto the stage

---

6   *Bereshit* 38:6–9.
7   Ibid., 30:15.

without a name, but simply referred to as "his [Moshe's] sister."[8] When she is first mentioned by name, much later in the narrative at the song by the Reed Sea, she is referred to as Aharon's sister.[9] To bring this full circle, in the genealogy of the Jewish people in the book of *Bemidbar*, she is referred to as their (Moshe *and* Aharon's) sister.[10]

Similarly, the comparative lack of pathos when Moshe and Aharon reunite after many years of separation[11] reveals a calm and unambivalent relationship. Absent is the falling on the neck and crying that marks the reunion of brothers and of fathers and sons in the book of *Bereshit*.[12] The crying and the carrying on that appear in the other stories are a response to feelings of loss and regret at what could have been. In all of those cases, mistakes had been made and opportunities had been missed. And, as is the way of such situations, the feelings of loss could be fully recognized only after the changes that had taken place in the other person had been observed. This, of course, could occur only at the point of reunion. Unlike the stories in *Bereshit*, the separation of Moshe and Aharon appears to have been preceded by harmony and a lack of complexity. Thus, whatever missed opportunities elapsed on account of their separation resulted from events outside their control. The outcome of all this was Moshe and Aharon's emotionally uncomplicated reunion.[13]

But this is just icing on the cake of a narrative that shows tremendous cooperation between siblings from day one. Instead of rivalry, we encounter a division of labor based on respective aptitudes on the one hand and Divine election on the other. Moshe is the ultimate leader and the primary connection to

---

8   *Shemot* 2:4. It is true that Moshe's parents are also described anonymously at this point, but they are also not described as Moshe's parents in the way that Miriam is described as Moshe's sister. Moreover, the Torah doesn't wait as long to reveal their names. See also Ramban on *Shemot* 2:1.

9   Ibid., 15:20–21.

10 *Bemidbar* 26:59.

11 *Shemot* 4:27.

12 *Bereshit* 33:4, 45:14 and 46:29.

13 The lack of complexity revealed in Moshe and Aharon's reunion could also be due to the lack of previous exposure to each other, Moshe having grown up largely out of his home. At the same time, that doesn't negate the fact that their reunion also reflects a lack of earlier conflict in comparison to the other stories.

God's will. Aharon serves as the great communicator, translating Moshe's message into human terms for both Jew and non-Jew.[14] (The priesthood, which is given over to Aharon, can also be seen as a mode of transmission of the Divine experience to the masses.) Finally – though we know less about her than we do about Moshe and Aharon – Miriam seems to provide a feminine dimension to the national leadership, displayed at the song by the Reed Sea.

The contrast between these siblings and the ones mentioned earlier deserves our attention. What is it that allowed the children of Amram to work together with such "brotherly" love when their predecessors did not?

One could point to Moshe's unique trait of modesty[15] as the main feature that preempted any feelings of jealousy among his siblings. After all, Moshe mightily resisted taking the mantle of leadership and, according to many, campaigned with God that his older brother should take the position instead.[16] Certainly, this characteristic must have played a major role in the unfolding of their cooperation.

Another direction we could explore is the effect of Egyptian enmity on Jewish unity on the whole of Moshe's generation. Indeed, when Moshe is still in Pharaoh's court and sees a fellow Jew being hit by an Egyptian, the text tells us that he saw "an Egyptian man hitting an Israelite man, from among [Moshe's] *brothers*."[17] The notion of closing ranks in the face of a common foe is well-known. But the text quickly reminds us that this is not a universal response. Immediately after this episode, we read of two Jews first fighting with each other and then subsequently rebuffing Moshe's attempt to settle the dispute. According to rabbinic tradition, it was actually these two fellow Jews who informed on Moshe, nearly causing his death at the hand of Pharaoh.[18]

In addition to the variables mentioned above, we also find a more historical process at play, whereby the mistakes of previous generations are slowly learned. It is precisely the conflict between Yosef and his brothers that brought

---

14 See *Targum Onkelos* on *Shemot* 7:2, who writes that Aharon served as Moshe's *meturgaman* (translator/public orator).

15 See Chapter 2.

16 Rashi, Ibn Ezra et al. on *Shemot* 4:13.

17 *Shemot* 2:11.

18 *Shemot Rabba* 1:31.

the Jews down to Egypt to begin with. Hence, it makes sense that unity among siblings is one of the prime reasons for their deliverance from Egypt – a sort of national "*tikkun*" for what had previously gone wrong.

(It should be pointed out that conflict between siblings will not become a thing of the past once we arrive at this point in Jewish history. Sibling conflict and rivalry will reappear many more times before we are finished with the Biblical chronicle, most famously in the narrative of David's children.[19])

It appears that several factors – none of which was likely the sole cause – came together to allow for the beautiful partnership between Moshe and his siblings. There may well be an additional factor that had a determinant effect on this unprecedented brotherly unity. Miriam's active concern for baby Moshe[20] is one example that leads us to the conclusion that the *achva* (brotherhood) of these siblings may have even preceded Moshe's birth. Returning to the idea of learning from earlier mistakes, we should also consider the converse – that the children of Amram derived significant sustenance from events that occurred before they were even born. Previously developed positive teachings of how brothers (and sisters) can live together amicably informed their unity.

The End of the Beginning

We need not look too far before the birth of Moshe to find the key. Perhaps the most important lesson about brotherhood in the entire Bible is found right before the beginning of the book of *Shemot* in the blessings that Ya'akov gives his children at the end of his life.[21] Though difficult to read and understand, their importance should not be underestimated. In fact, they serve as a type of conclusion to the entire book of *Bereshit* – not only as the end of the saga of the Jewish family that would go down to Egypt and there become a nation, but also as a solution to the problem that plagues almost all of the major characters throughout the book and is the subject of this chapter, namely, how to forge a harmonious relationship with one's potential competitors.[22]

19 See *II Shmuel* 13:22–29 and *I Melachim* 1.
20 *Shemot* 2:5–9.
21 *Bereshit* 49:8–26.
22 See also R. Jonathan Sacks, *One People* (London: Littman Library, 1993), pp.

Even before the blessings, Ya'akov was already aware that not all sibling rivalry is due to ill will and the problem would not be solved by simply looking to blame one of the siblings for the conflict. The conflict between his children – as well as between his primary wives – proved that sibling rivalry and its manifestations does not emanate only from the presence of a "bad seed" such as Yishmael and Esav, but also among individuals that Ya'akov believed to be righteous.

By the time Ya'akov eventually finds a resolution to this issue and distributes the blessings, it comes as the culmination of his own experiences of struggle with his own brother. As we argued in *Redeeming Relevance in Genesis*, it is not clear that Ya'akov and Esav couldn't have worked out their issues with each other. And had they been able to come to an understanding, they could have possibly cooperated on a variety of fronts. Thus, Ya'akov may well have pondered the wasted time and energy that he needed to devote to the affairs of the world – affairs which could have likely been handled more efficiently by his brother.[23] Instead, not only could Ya'akov not turn to his brother for assistance, he had to be on his guard from him to make sure that he would not be injured.

Presumably, this was now a problem that Ya'akov saw recurring with his own children, if on a more moderate scale. If he may not have seen the extent of the problem when he sent Yosef to find his brothers,[24] Ya'akov was certainly aware that there were ill feelings between the two parties. In fact, when the brothers proposed to kill Yosef, there was a marked similarity to Esav wanting to kill Ya'akov. In both stories, the point of climax in the struggle for the family succession was when the younger brother is sent into exile to clear the path for the older *heir apparent*. This *déjà vu* alone would be enough reason for Ya'akov to think seriously about how he would prevent history from repeating itself, as he must have done before giving the blessings. Looking more closely at them and at the subsequent lack of conflict between the brothers, we can see that Ya'akov had such a harmonious resolution in mind.

199–203, for an alternative, albeit similar, understanding of this theme.

23   See Seforno on *Bereshit* 27:29, who claims that this was exactly Yitzchak's intention in his desire to bless Esav.

24   *Bereshit* 37:13–14.

Through the blessings to his children, Ya'akov was the first to explicitly realize and subsequently formulate the idea that *specialization* of tasks is the key to group cooperation. Granted, this idea is already latent from the beginning, when the first two brothers pursue different and potentially symbiotic livelihoods. Nonetheless, it is never unambiguously formulated until Ya'akov blesses his children. With his carefully individualized and complementary blessings, Ya'akov provides an important teaching for his progeny – that leadership is only one of many indispensable roles that must be taken for a family to maximize its success. There is a need for the merchant as well as the scholar as well as the leader.[25] If one role may be more glamorous than another, specialization allows each brother to take on an essential function on behalf of the group. This strategy for familial harmony is as simple as it is brilliant. It enables each family member to excel in what he (or she) does best, thereby allowing for self-actualization, while defusing concern about being beaten out by a rival sibling. Furthermore, it creates interdependence, which results in a team scenario. Simply put, if my teammate does well, it benefits not only him, but me as well.

Indeed, finding a modus vivendi for siblings can serve as a paradigm for how to deal with other competitors as well. The direct rivalry for the same goods produced by an inheritance engenders a *need* for working things out that doesn't exist with the same intensity among strangers. This need stimulates the creation of a model of cooperation, the urgency of which does not generally exist outside a family. Moreover, the bonds of familial love and shared history provide further impetus to construct this model. In short, the family provides fertile ground for the creation of a universal scheme of cooperation between independent competitors. And it is just such a scheme that comes to fruition after Ya'akov's blessings.

---

25 See Rabbi S. R. Hirsch, "Lessons from Jacob and Esau," in *Collected Writings of Rabbi Samson Raphael Hirsch,* vol. vii (Jerusalem: Feldheim Publishers, 1997), pp. 325–27.

Fraternity and Equality

The relationship between Moshe and his siblings is challenged at one famous juncture – the complaint made by Aharon and Miriam concerning Moshe's apparent separation from his wife.[26] The language of the complaint is highly unclear and as a result has been interpreted in many different ways. What is clear, however, is that God is not pleased with how Aharon and Miriam related to their brother there.

In their conversation, Aharon and Miriam compare themselves with Moshe. It appears that they feel there is no difference between them and Moshe since they too are prophets or, in the context of this chapter in the Torah, partners in Israel's mission at this seminal juncture in Jewish history. Moreover, as suggested by the Midrash,[27] their critique of Moshe is rooted in a comparison with other prophets who had come before them. Moshe's action vis-a-vis his wife was hard for his siblings to accept since it lacked any precedent. Whatever its motivation, Aharon and Miriam's conversation shattered the unity that had epitomized the relationship between the three up until this point.

Yet upon further consideration, we shall see that the disagreement between Moshe and his siblings represents a necessary fine-tuning of the strategy they inherited from Ya'akov's blessing. The unity created by a team's division of labor can give a false sense of parity – that since all the parts are necessary, they are also all equal. In our case, Miriam and Aharon felt free to use the same measuring stick on their brother that they used on themselves; they thought they could determine his value based on their own.

Of course, all necessary parts are equal in the sense that the greater organism cannot function if it lacks any one of them; this level of equality which gives individual self-worth is what makes the strategy work in the first place. Nonetheless, that does not make all the parts of truly equal importance. Some may play a more significant role than others. For example, even if a person

26 *Bemidbar* 12:1–13. Though it is not clear from the text, we will follow the rabbinic interpretation that Moshe's elevated level of prophecy led to a permanent separation from his wife (see *Tanchuma*, Parashat Tzav 13).

27 *Sifrei* on *Bemidbar* 12:2.

cannot (normally) survive without a stomach, it would be difficult to argue that the stomach is as important as the brain. That is because the brain fulfills tasks of greater consequence than the stomach. Indeed, our brains are what define us as human beings. I have yet to meet anyone (and hope never to meet anyone!) whose stomach defines his identity.

When God makes this point and tells Aharon that Moshe is a different type of prophet and therefore not to be compared with anyone else,[28] Aharon quickly internalizes it. We see this immediately when Aharon addresses his younger brother as "my master Moshe" when requesting the latter to pray for Miriam's recovery.[29] Aharon's submission to Moshe's superiority[30] implied by his form of address tells us that he accepted God's rebuke wholeheartedly. Granted, Aharon has good reason to accept it, as it came from God Himself, but we know that when the personality flaw of jealousy is behind a complaint, it can be so self-destructive that even Divine intervention is not enough to convince the guilty party to cease and desist. In our case, however, Aharon accepts and immediately adjusts to God's view regarding the nature of his relationship with his brother. Moshe, for his part, also doesn't appear to be upset by the incident, quickly responding to Aharon's request to pray for Miriam – whom God was punishing for assuming herself to be his equal.

As seen from the behavior of all concerned, the source of the mistake appears to be misjudgment rather than envy. That Miriam and Aharon weren't aware of Moshe's singularity may actually tell us that Moshe wasn't aware of it either. He knew that his level of prophecy was greater than that of his siblings, but that doesn't mean he knew that the role that it allowed him to play was more important than the roles of his brother and sister.

The unusual disagreement that we have just discussed is the only exception to an otherwise harmonious sibling dynamic. Once it is over, our trio returns to the unified team they were previously. What occurred is what we should expect from a solid working relationship. When disagreements occur, they often provide the impetus to make the relationship even better. In this case, a

28 *Bemidbar* 12:5–9.
29 Ibid., 12:11.
30 See R. Yitzchak S. Reggio (Perush haYashar) on *Bemidbar* 12:11.

possible misconception about the nature of a team was clarified. Specifically, the players learned that though teamwork may lead to harmony and maximum self-expression, it does not lead to a state of perfect equality.[31]

Of Fraternity and Fratricide

Before we round out our discussion of Moshe and Aharon, it is worth reviewing Aharon's use of the term "my master" for Moshe. First, it is not common to see any older brother using this term regarding a younger brother – even if we can readily think of Moshe as Aharon's master. Moreover, Aharon uses the term in reference to Moshe only one time earlier: strategically when Moshe blames him for his role in producing the golden calf.[32] There too, Aharon is acknowledging his inferiority to Moshe; he had just aided in the performance of a sin while his brother was involved in the highest communion with God. But if this was really an acknowledgement of inferiority, then why does Aharon go back to viewing himself as an equal to Moshe in the later section that we just discussed?

Aharon's culpability in the golden calf incident is not clear-cut. As Moshe's go-between in the midst of an incipient rebellion, he had very few options. Had Moshe been in his brother's place, would he have fared any better? It is precisely because of his willingness to be among the people in their worst moments as well as in their best moments that Aharon was mourned by the people more than Moshe.[33] That being the case, Aharon's first use of "my master" might have a tinge of irony – i.e., it is easy for the master who does not

31 Indeed, the concept of complete equality is, to a large extent, a modern myth. At base level, it is true that every human being is endowed with a sacred Divine image and it is precisely because of this that one life may not be sacrificed for another (*Sanhedrin* 74a). At the same time, it is plainly evident that some people play more vital roles than others and for this reason Jewish law proposes a hierarchy concerning the ransoming of captives, returning lost objects, etc. (*Horayot* 13a). That being the case, teamwork should not be mistaken for absolute equality.

32 *Shemot* 32:22.

33 *Pirkei deRabbi Eliezer* 17, based on the comparison of *Bemidbar* 20:29 and *Devarim* 34:8.

need to deal with the people to criticize, but perhaps, as the rabbis were later to say, one should not judge until he has been in the same situation.[34]

Whether the irony was intended or not, the simple message of Aharon's subservience to Moshe becomes blurred by its problematic context. For even if Aharon was later to see that his role was not as central as Moshe's, this may not have yet been clear to him – all the more so since it was Aharon and not Moshe who appeared to have the more difficult job.

Consequently, the expression "my master" used by Aharon after he is rebuked by Moshe appears as an alternative way of saying "I confess my mistake." The fiasco with the golden calf could have been an opportunity for Aharon to internalize his inferiority to his almost superhuman brother. Still the Torah hints that this did not happen until later, when he would use the expression again – this time with more conviction. In other words, the scene with the golden calf opens up the discussion of their lack of equality and the argument over Moshe's wife closes it. The Torah frames this subnarrative with Aharon's unusual use of the phrase "my master" for his younger brother.

If the scene with the golden calf opens one topic, it apparently concludes another. For it is in this context that Moshe teaches us another stark limitation of brotherhood. When Moshe tells the Levites to kill anyone who was directly involved in worshiping the golden calf, he tells them that this includes their brothers and their relatives[35] – an obvious redundancy,[36] Moshe may have mentioned the word "brothers" to send a chilling warning to his own brother, whose behavior he had implicitly just censored. That is to say, Moshe is passing judgment here on the admissibility of fratricide under very limited conditions.

As mentioned earlier, the theme of fratricide is already quite familiar from the book of *Bereshit*. We see it with Kayin and Hevel, and it reappears when Esav wants to kill Ya'akov and again when the brothers plot to kill Yosef. So long as fratricide is even within the realm of the possible, we cannot expect brothers to be able to work together. However, once we reach the end of *Bereshit* and have progressed to the paradigm of brotherly cooperation, we

34 *Avot* 2:4.
35 *Shemot* 32:27.
36 See Ohr haChaim on *Shemot* 32:27, who notices this redundancy.

might easily think that killing one's brother is unacceptable under any circumstances and that the death penalty is reserved only for strangers (a question closely related to one that the Talmud actually takes up regarding whether an executioner can put his own parent to death[37]).

Moshe proclaims that in the same way society cannot function without cooperation between disparate member units, it also cannot function when that cooperation results in a willingness to look the other way when a member of the "team" acts in an immoral or lawless fashion. Indeed, the slogan, "My country, right or wrong," is far from the Jewish prophetic tradition of harsh national self-criticism.

An individual is not expected to punish himself – it is incongruent with his God-given instinct for self-preservation. While this instinct can sometimes also be legitimate on the national level, Moshe teaches us that there is a need to distinguish between self-dispensation and extending that dispensation to other members of the team. Whereas the former is an intrinsic part of God's design of man, the latter goes beyond that purview.

The upshot is that even if we need to work with our rivals and view them as members of our team, this should not include exempting them from the strictures of the law and from its enforcement. A team must be willing to sacrifice its members when they do not conform to the moral demands required for a properly functioning society of a humanity whose job it is to perfect itself in response to the Divine call.

◆   ◆   ◆

The lessons from Moshe, Aharon and Miriam go well beyond their immediate context. On some level, Amram's children show us how to create an orderly society, because the relationship among siblings – ultimately independent and competing individuals who must somehow learn to live together – is really a microcosm of society at large.

Of course, one could readily argue that this paradigm will never completely be applicable at the global level. Even if we could fathom an entire nation working as a team through specialization, its citizens would still feel

---

37 *Sanhedrin* 85a-b.

rivalry with other nations competing for the same zero-sum goods. Indeed, in the next chapter, we will discuss a different paradigm that will allow us to overcome the very real obstacles created by nationalism. Nonetheless, the current model of an extended family or nation that views itself communally as an interdependent team allows us to fathom the contours of a truly global consciousness. In this way, the seeds are planted for the peace of the messianic era, wherein "nation will not lift up their sword against another nation."

Another problem that already exists even on the national level is that the larger the community, the less personal it is and, as a result, the less we identify with it. Truly, the modern nation is exponentially larger than the twelve families that first comprised the ancient Jewish nation. But as in other metaphors created by the Jewish tradition for things too intangible to comprehend,[38] this model is meant to give us a sense of what community should feel like even if we can't completely feel it today.

As shown in the book of *Bereshit*, the main alternative to brotherly cooperation is living apart. In the global village we now inhabit, however, there is almost no way to live apart from others. Once this is the case, the only option becomes the other possibility we saw in *Bereshit*, namely murder. Thus, as the stakes become greater, we have a greater obligation to understand and practice the paradigm of brotherhood exemplified by the Moshe-Aharon-Miriam family team.

---

38 For example, speaking of (the sensual joys of) Shabbat as a taste of the world to come (*Berachot* 57b).

CHAPTER 5

Yitro: The First Other

🉲 The problem . . . is that we don't believe we are as much alike as we are . . . If we saw each other as more alike, we might be very eager to join in one big human family . . . and to care about that family the way we care about our own.

(Mitch Albom quoting Morrie Schwartz, *Tuesdays with Morrie*)

IN THE PREVIOUS chapter, we discussed a basic model of familial cooperation that provides a structure for communal living. A related issue that has not yet been addressed is relationships between communities. These are ultimately more problematic than the relations within a family or a community. Indeed, most wars are not fought within a communal unit but rather between *different* groupings.

Short of a utopian messianic scenario, mankind will always be divided by culture, geography and the like. And it is these separations that allow us to exclude most of the world's inhabitants from what we see as our own interests or, as we termed it in the previous chapter, our "team." To go from this inevitably human perspective of insiders and outsiders to the fighting of wars often does not take much.[1] Two groups both desperately wanting the same thing have

---

1   In this regard, the phrasing of the commandment to love *reacha* (your friend or neighbor; *Vayikra* 19:18) appropriately limits the object of one's love to something accessible to the average man. *Reacha* limits the obligation to a person in one's community and not to every person on the face of the earth. Granted, we are also commanded to love the stranger (*ger*), but this too has been traditionally understood to

very little means by which to come to an agreement, so long as they see each other as foreigners.

The fact that human history may be seen as an almost uninterrupted string of wars and conflicts shows that we are in even more pressing need for a workable ethic between communities than we are for the team ethic discussed in the previous chapter. Thus, we will certainly want to look at some of the many strangers who appear together in the Torah.

No less than his modern counterpart, the Biblical Jew was part of a small and vulnerable community. As such, necessity required that he have dealings with foreigners. To take the earliest example, Avraham needed to interact with Pharaoh,[2] Avimelech,[3] Efron,[4] and the various leaders involved in the Sodomite wars.[5] Happily, most of these encounters ended up positively enough. Thus, at first glance, they give us early hope for the coexistence of nations. At the same time, a more careful examination of these encounters reveals that all of them are characterized by a palpable sense of *quid pro quo*. Pharaoh is willing to give Avraham back his wife and even to enrich him because he has already seen that Avraham has unusual powers that can be used against those who mistreat him. Likewise, Efron is gracious to him only in order to help him secure a very lucrative deal for the burial plot being solicited. For his part, Avraham likely realizes that even with all of the Divine aid he receives, he is ultimately alone. That being the case, he must somehow get along with the lords of whatever place he finds himself.

It is fairly intuitive that when common interests are found, there is certainly room for banquets and deals. But what happens when interests don't overlap? After all, it is obvious that the interests of any two groups are rarely identical. Precisely for that reason, then, Avraham does not provide us with a highly useful paradigm of how to deal with the stranger and we will therefore

---

be speaking only about the stranger in our midst. Moreover, this latter command is one that comes with a certain emphasis in the text, indicating its difficulty. (See Chapter 7, note 12, for elaboration on the connection between a commandment's emphasis and its difficulty.)

2   *Bereshit* 12:14–20.
3   Ibid., 20.
4   Ibid., 23:3–19.
5   Ibid., 14:10–24.

need to look further to find a model of peaceful coexistence between different groups, specifically when there is no obvious convergence of interests.

To help us find such a model, we will turn our attention to the most blatant contrast in the Ya'akov and Moshe narratives described in Chapter 3 – their fathers-in-law.

The Fathers-in-Law: Lavan and Yitro

In the same way that it is difficult to find two more similar stories than the respective exiles of Ya'akov and Moshe,[6] it is equally difficult to find two more disparate parallels than the roles played in these stories by their respective fathers-in-law.[7] Whereas Lavan seems to do something disagreeable every step of the way, Yitro does just the opposite, constantly providing help and support to his son-in-law. Ya'akov has to ask to marry one of Lavan's daughters,[8] whereas Yitro *offers* Zipporah to Moshe as his bride.[9] Not only that, Lavan makes the terms of the marriage agreement almost unbearable;[10] in the case of Moshe, we don't hear of any formal terms whatsoever. Most significantly, when Ya'akov asks to leave, we see Lavan trying repeatedly to foil his desires.[11] Regarding Moshe, he is not only given permission but an apparent blessing as well.[12] On the one hand, Lavan runs after Ya'akov in what could be understood as an effort to kidnap the wives and the children, whom Lavan describes as his own.[13] Yitro, on the other hand, runs after Moshe for just the opposite

---

6 See Chapter 3.

7 For our present purposes, we are assuming that the various names for the man referred to as Moshe's father-in-law (i.e. Yitro, Re'uel, Chovev) all describe the same person, whom we will, for simplicity's sake, call Yitro. While this point is a matter of debate and there are those who suggest that the various names refer to different people, most of the relevant citations are, in any case, from sections where the father-in-law is explicitly referred to as Yitro.

8 *Bereshit* 29:18.

9 *Shemot* 2:21.

10 *Bereshit* 29:26–7.

11 Ibid., 30:25–35, 31:22–24.

12 *Shemot* 4:18.

13 *Bereshit* 31:43.

reason – to bring his son-in-law's children and wife back to him.[14] Finally, when Lavan catches up with Ya'akov, he tries to impose his own religious preferences on his son-in-law, making sure that their non-belligerence pact makes reference to his own god as well as the God of Ya'akov.[15] In comparison, when Yitro finds Moshe in the desert, he makes the decision to offer sacrifices to his son-in-law's God alone and to leave sacrifices to his own gods for a more appropriate time.[16]

The Torah further emphasizes the difference between the two stories by constantly referring to Yitro as Moshe's father-in-law, while Ya'akov's father-in-law, Lavan, although mentioned far more frequently than Yitro, is not described as such even once. Instead, when we need clarification of his identity, we hear that he is an Aramean, the brother of Rivka or the son of Betuel. Although the Torah generally speaks about Moshe's relatives in relation to him (i.e., Moshe's sister, Moshe's brother, etc.), still, the stark contrast between the Torah's repeated identification of Yitro as a father-in-law and of Lavan as everything but a father-in-law is far too blatant to be unrelated to the discussion at hand. Hence, Lavan serves as a foil to Yitro: he is not called Ya'akov's father-in-law because he has not earned that title, even if his daughters are married to Ya'akov. To see what is required for that title, the Torah has us wait until we come to Yitro. Lavan must first show us what a father-in-law should not be in order for Yitro to eventually illustrate what a true father-in-law needs to be.

It is worth noting that the entire Bible describes only one other man as a father-in-law – the anonymous father of the concubine of Giv'ah.[17] There too, the father-in-law is notably benevolent in his treatment of his daughter's

---

14 *Shemot* 18:1–6.

15 *Bereshit* 31:53.

16 Of course Yitro's sacrificing only to God would be a foregone conclusion if he himself had completely converted to the Jewish faith, as indicated by many rabbinic statements. We will explain later, however, that such a reading doesn't seem to fit well with the text's simple meaning, nor does it seem to be a consensus position among the sages. As a result, we will assume that Yitro had not completely left idolatry at this time and that he made a conscious choice to worship only the Israelite God in Moshe's presence.

17 *Shofetim* 19:1–10. Whether the Torah, or the Bible as a whole, uses the correspond-

husband. Specifically, he rejoices when he sees his son-in-law, he feeds him and gives him drink, he beseeches him to prolong his visit and, ominously, not to leave when it is not safe. He is perhaps even more remarkable for lavishing benevolence on a somewhat murky character who, in any case, takes the daughter only as a concubine and not as a full wife. If, of all the many fathers-in-law in the Bible, only Yitro and he are singled out, it makes us think that they are the only ones the Bible feels deserve this designation. That is, they are the only ones who spell out the Biblical vision of a true father-in-law. And if we are to judge from these two men – as it appears that we should – that vision ultimately consists of someone who shows deep concern for his son-in-law's welfare.

The Stranger Who Marries Our Daughter

Even though we might assume that the standard relationship between father-in-law and son-in-law is basically harmonious, we shouldn't take it for granted. By reading the story of Lavan and Ya'akov, we can better appreciate the natural opposition that can exist in the relationship.

When Lavan first agrees to take Ya'akov on as a son-in-law, he already couches his graceless agreement in words of resentment at the whole institution. "It is better that I give her to you than that I should give her to another man,"[18] he says, as if this is the better of two evils. Indeed, by the end of the story, when Lavan catches up with his fugitive son-in-law, his feelings become quite transparent. Referring to that which has accrued to Ya'akov, Lavan unabashedly claims that "the daughters are my daughters and the sons are my sons and the flocks are my flocks and everything that you see is *mine!*"[19] In effect, Lavan's depiction of a son-in-law is that of a culturally sanctioned thief. Even more, this is a thief who steals that which is most precious. Put otherwise, taking on a son-in-law is a sort of grueling compromise that one must make in order to provide for a daughter's needs. From this perspective, if one's

---

ing word "*chatan*" to mean a son-in-law with similar intentionality is less clear. See, for example, *Bereshit* 19:12–14.
18 *Bereshit* 29:19.
19 Ibid., 31:43.

sons are an asset that will add to one's wealth, daughters are only as a liability. In fact, from this callously commercial perspective, they are a net loss.

In contrast, Yitro gives us a completely different conception of the relationship between father-in-law and son-in-law. While Yitro is more circumspect about what motivates him, the honor granted him by Moshe and the Jewish people shows that there is more than a little wisdom to Yitro's policy, even if only from a pragmatic point of view.

In place of the resentment that Lavan shows toward his son-in-law at every step of the way, Yitro immediately shows respect for his son-in-law's independence – a respect which may well be the most vital element in such a relationship. Shortly after we are introduced to Yitro, he recognizes Moshe's autonomy by granting his son-in-law the right to live away from him.[20] As mentioned earlier, Lavan's resistance to Ya'akov's request to leave is in stark contrast to the blessing Yitro gives to Moshe when he makes the same request. Likewise, the concubine's father mentioned above also acquiesces to his son-in-law's (in this case, unwise) desire to leave toward dusk. That the son-in-law is able to leave freely despite his father-in-law's opposition only reinforces the notion that a proper father-in-law accepts his son-in-law's right to make his own decisions. The father-in-law can advise otherwise, as he does in this case, but he cannot infringe on the son-in-law's prerogative to make the decision for himself and his wife.[21]

This respect immediately signals a relationship of equals. Such equality is certainly not obvious, given the father-in-law's usually more powerful standing in society and the filial obligation that the son-in-law's partner – the married daughter – still needs to fulfill. This is all the more true in the case of Yitro, who is not only Moshe's father-in-law, but initially also his boss (something

---

20 *Shemot* 4:18.

21 The Torah emphasizes the centrality of acceding to such a request in an interesting twist, where it is Yitro who is requesting to take leave of Moshe (*Bemidbar* 10:30). At that point, the tables are turned and the father-in-law is the more vulnerable guest – all the more so since Moshe's stature has eclipsed that of his father-in-law. Recognizing the basic equality between them, Moshe also limits himself to trying to convince Yitro to stay and steers clear of anything more coercive.

equally true about the relationship of Ya'akov and Lavan, as emphasized in Chapter 3).

The equal footing that Yitro gives Moshe is the only attitude that the son-in-law can comfortably accept from someone who is ultimately a stranger, as we will soon explain. For being a stranger is at least partially defined by not having any prior relationship, hierarchical or otherwise. This holds true even when that stranger becomes a relative through marriage.

Treating a stranger as an equal requires far-sightedness. It requires the understanding that when strangers work together it usually ends up being to everyone's benefit, in spite of the personal loss of status or property that it might originally entail for one of them. Investment in the future always requires giving things up in the here and now. Apparently armed with this knowledge, Yitro exhibits a willingness to freely give to his son-in-law.

The Other

Yitro truly gives much to Moshe, but he is best remembered for the advice he gave Moshe to appoint judges below him. For our purposes, what is most important here is the manner in which Yitro respects his son-in-law's autonomy even as he bestows his wisdom upon him. He does this by expressing his valuable solution in an even more valuable manner. By conditioning his suggestion on Divine confirmation,[22] he makes sure that it will be acceptable to his son-in-law's religious sensibilities.[23]

This last point may be most significant. Through it, we see Yitro's advice expressed in a way that shows a willingness to see the world from a foreign perspective which is radically different from his own. Ultimately, this willingness is the true litmus test of whether one can truly cooperate with the stranger. It follows that the paradigm of cross-cultural cooperation given to us by Moshe and Yitro is dependent upon our willingness to extend ourselves be-

---

22 *Shemot* 18:23.
23 Obviously, there are limits to this. Though we can be sensitive to the religious sensitivities of the other, Jewish law demands an uncompromising stance towards any foreign religious practice or belief deemed detrimental to our mission as Jews.

yond our most valued communal attitudes and beliefs. (Obviously, we are not discussing an openness to the other so extreme as to become self-destructive.)

We learn from Yitro that perhaps only when we are motivated to listen to the other and to see the legitimacy of the opposing perspective do we open ourselves up to the other's resultant needs and demands. Presumably, at that point, competition for resources as well as affection takes on a completely different hue.

◆ ◆ ◆

Of course, the willingness to have empathy for *this particular stranger* has its impetus in a father's continued concern for his daughter after she moves out of her parents' home. This is most clearly illustrated by the description of the other benevolent father-in-law mentioned above. There, the text repeatedly reminds us of the obvious fact that he is the *"father of the maiden"* as well as the father-in-law.[24] Though less pronounced, Yitro's interest in Moshe is also grounded in his being the "father of the maiden." His main mission in going to Moshe in the desert is to take care of his daughter by bringing her back to her husband. Thus, the concern of the Biblical father-in-law remains rooted in his concern for his own offspring even as it also extends to her husband.

At the same time, the son-in-law still remains more a stranger than true family. Indeed, the Biblical son-in-law remains only indirectly connected to his wife's father. Economically, the in-law is not much better than any other foreigner, receiving no direct inheritance. In other areas as well, the bond is tenuous and impermanent – it only truly exists when the blood relative is still alive. Hence, the novelty of Ruth is that she decides to continue the bond with her mother-in-law, Naomi, even after Ruth's husband has died. That this is not expected is succinctly heard in Naomi's words to her daughters-in-law, "Why should you go with me? Do I have more sons in my womb that they should be husbands to you?"[25]

Yitro's geographic and cultural distance from Moshe further demonstrates

24 See Malbim and Me'am Loez on *Shofetim* 19:13–14, who point out this unusual double epithet but give somewhat different explanations.
25 *Ruth* 1:11–12.

the very real separation between parents-in-law and children-in-law. One example is when Yitro rebuffs Moshe's attempt to have him go with them to the Land of Israel. His graciousness notwithstanding, Moshe also makes it clear that there will always be separation between the two. In fact, Moshe had already hinted at this to Yitro earlier. When Moshe asks to go back to Egypt, he asks to return to his *brothers*,[26] a term that clearly excludes Yitro. This is emphasized a second time when Moshe tries to convince Yitro to stay with the Jews – Moshe speaks about *us* and *you*.[27] For his part, Yitro reflects back the knowledge that he will remain an outsider, emphasizing that Midian is his home.[28] In other words, both protagonists know that whether Yitro chooses to go and live with the Jews or not, he will never be a member of Moshe's in-group. The question of Yitro's joining the Jews is one of proximity, not one of true unity. For there are distinctions that can be bridged and there are those that cannot. The bond that Yitro and the Jews can create is a real one, but it is not meant to remove the distinction between those within and those without.

An Unlikely Association

One may wonder why we don't see the paradigm of Yitro and Moshe earlier in the Torah. It may simply be that the right combination of characters does not precede them. At the same time, it seems purposeful that the paradigm of how to treat others is set among two individuals who are more than moderately different from each other. In this case, it is not just the story of two people who are not part of the same community – it is the story of two men who lead radically dissimilar lives. Reinforcing our sense of intentionality, the Torah clearly emphasizes some of the major differences between Moshe and Yitro.

Here, the generational gap that almost always separates fathers-in-law from their sons-in-law is compounded by an important cultural hurdle. The Torah repeatedly tells us that Yitro is a Midianite. It tells us this not only when Yitro first meets Moshe, but also when he and Moshe are reunited – showing us that

---

26 *Shemot* 4:18.
27 *Bemidbar* 10:29.
28 Ibid., verse 30.

his national identity is not altered by his familial connection with Moshe. In fact, the Torah may be indicating just the opposite. When the two are still together in Midian, Yitro is described as "his father-in-law, *Kohen Midian*." Later when they reunite, the order is switched and he is now *Kohen Midian*, Moshe's father-in-law," telling us that Yitro doesn't just keep the identity of *Kohen Midian*, he apparently becomes even more entrenched in it.[29] At a time when religion and nationality were identical, Yitro's retaining his Midianite identity bears a critical significance. More than just a common Midianite, as "*Kohen Midian*," he is a man of standing in the national and *religious* community of his birth.

The simple meaning of the word *kohen* is priest – exactly how it is understood by some of the early rabbinic sources.[30] That would make him a minister in the idolatrous cult of his native culture, something no doubt anathema to his son-in-law. His statement, "Now I know that God is greater than other gods [*elohim*],"[31] only gives us more reason to think that he never renounced his polytheistic beliefs. Furthermore, Yitro lives among idolaters and returns to them[32] after being invited to join the monotheistic Jewish

---

29 Of course, this can also be attributed to Moshe's absence; whatever influence Moshe had upon him waned when the two men were apart.

30 See the first opinion in the *Mechilta* on *Shemot* 18:1. That being said, it is also true that the second opinion in the *Mechilta* as well as the *Targum Onkelos* try to deflect the negative implications of such a term by translating the word according to its secondary meaning, leader, as per its apparent usage in *II Shmuel* 8:18.

31 *Shemot* 18:11. While the same claim could be made about the Israelites' rhetorical question in the song at the sea (ibid., 15:11), "Who is like You among the gods (*elim*)?", the fact that it is phrased as a question makes it easier to interpret otherwise. (Whereas a statement is based in a speaker's frame of reference, a question is directed more toward that of one's interlocutor. Though the Jews are not speaking to anyone in particular, it is possible that they are addressing all of mankind who, for most of history, held polytheistic beliefs.)

32 Even if Yitro's return to Midian is not made totally clear from *Bemidbar* 10:29–33, this is certainly his explicitly expressed original intention, and many of the classical commentators conclude that the Torah would have let us know if he changed his mind and decided to stay with the Jews. See, for example, Abarbanel and Ohr haChaim. See also Seforno, who holds that Yitro went back to Midian, but agreed to send his own children with the Jews.

people.[33] Simply put, there could be no greater gap between the man of God and the polytheistic priest.

Whatever connection Yitro does share with the Jewish people has very little to do with the Jews themselves; it is rather based on his relationship with his daughter and, through her (and through his grandchildren), with Moshe. Another example from the text reminds us about how Yitro viewed his world. When the Torah recounts Yitro hearing about the deliverance of the Jewish people, it explains that he heard "what God did *for Moshe* and for Israel."[34] That this order is not coincidental is reinforced later by a similar passage wherein Yitro advises Moshe to appoint other judges, explaining that otherwise, first Moshe will become worn out and then, secondly, the Jewish people will also become worn out.[35] Indeed, the author of *Sifrei* underscores the critical importance of Moshe in Yitro's bond with the Jews. He writes that Moshe tried to give Yitro the mistaken impression that he, Moshe, was also destined to cross over into Israel, because otherwise Yitro would immediately refuse to go there himself.[36] In other words, Yitro's link to the Jews is contingent on Moshe, and not on any broader connection to the Jewish nation.

In short, by stressing the gap that exists between Yitro and Moshe, the Torah drives home that their affable relationship has little to with anything they share intrinsically. Keeping the story of Ruth in mind, we can presume that Yitro had the option of making the relationship with his son-in-law's people/religion both fundamental and permanent. The differences between him and his son-in-law could have been bridged.

---

33 Indeed, the rabbinic voices that would like to understand otherwise are hard put to explain this behavior, speculating that he went back to Midian to convert his countrymen. Such statements notwithstanding, had Yitro actually converted, one wonders why neither Biblical nor rabbinic texts discuss his conversion *per se*, in the same way as we find with Ruth. At the same time, that doesn't mean that we should discount him from being a righteous gentile. According to many early and late rabbinic authorities, it is enough that he gives sacrifices to the God of Israel, at least as one of several deities that he worships, in order for him to be considered a righteous gentile and not an idolater.

34 *Shemot* 18:1.

35 Ibid., verse 18.

36 *Sifrei* on *Bemidbar* 10:29.

At the same time, had Yitro chosen the path of Ruth and melded into Moshe's family and nation, the relationship would have less application to the broader global community. It would have been a story of two former strangers who combined their fortunes to create a new, unified community. If, however, Yitro does remain an idolater and yet still shows true love and concern for Moshe, we are given what might be the best window into the Torah's vision of positive interaction with the "other." Hence, Yitro and Moshe signal a paradigm of strangers who remain strangers. They continue to see the world through the lenses of very different cultures. And yet, in spite of what separates them, they are able to work together and show genuine concern for each other.

◆　◆　◆

Procreation does not automatically require the institution of marriage – reproduction in the animal kingdom is rarely accompanied by anything that we could construe as matrimony. Alternatively, God could have created a world in which incestuous relationships were preferable. Instead we have been given an institution which forces us to create bonds with strangers and move out of our immediate family circle. And this it does in two ways. Primarily, it makes us fasten our most significant interpersonal bond with someone we often meet only as an adult, long after we have developed our own character, attitudes and values. But perhaps even more important for the current discussion is the secondary level: it forces us to create relationships that are created with our spouse's family. When two people wed, they create new nuclear communities; when parents-in-law and children in-law are brought together, they create more complex and thus more difficult networks of interpersonal concern. These inevitable networks are what force us to deal with strangers. And in learning how to deal appropriately with such strangers – as well as others beyond the family purview – we are well advised to take our cue from the Jewish tradition's première father-in-law.

Through Yitro and Moshe we see how to relate to the in-law. Though our relatives by marriage can be dissimilar to us, we meet in the realm of common human concern. In fact, sometimes this is the only thing that we have in common. At the same time, it is precisely this shared concern that allows us to feel what is most articulately described in German as "*mitleid*," literally, pain *with*.

When I share my child's pain with her husband, we experience the same vicarious pain together. In that sense, we both experience something more similar to each other than that which we share with the daughter and wife we both love. The awareness that a stranger can share so completely in my own emotions vividly opens me up to my commonality with him – one even more basic than what I can appreciate via a common culture or religion. We all love and we all hurt, we all have needs and aspirations. More important than anything else, we are all created in the Divine image.

◆ ◆ ◆

Since the humanity we share with all people is usually taken for granted, we normally focus on what separates us. The things that separate us from other communities are very real – the problem is that they prevent us from seeing the many more things that we have in common with all men. Appreciating this baseline commonality is the most critical ingredient in our ability to work with people on "other teams."

In sum, the son-in-law is a stranger who captures our interest even as he remains distinct from us. He is one step away from the anonymity of the total stranger. Through the prism of this chosen stranger, however, we learn to act toward the total stranger. Indeed, through this prism we understand that *there is ultimately no such thing as a true stranger.*

CHAPTER 6

Clothing Aharon

W E SOMETIMES FORGET about the pervasiveness of clothing in our lives: along with food and shelter, clothing represents our most basic acquired necessity. And of the three, it is the only one that constantly accompanies us throughout our waking hours and that distinguishes us from animals.

But clothing is much more than a vital need. Beyond keeping us warm and protected, its most common functions are to protect our sense of privacy and to communicate various personal or communal messages. From "I am wealthy" to "I am not concerned with externals" – and everything in between – messages are communicated both intentionally and subconsciously via what we wear. Even the most basic aspect of our clothing, its very color, can generate a reaction in others. The Talmud aptly, if somewhat shockingly, illustrates this when it tells us about one of the sages who was so incensed to see a certain woman wearing a red dress that he ripped it right off of her.[1]

In light of its many important tasks, clothing serves as a sort of extension of our very selves. In fact, we often get so accustomed to wearing our clothes that we forget that we are wearing ultimately *foreign* objects. But foreignness notwithstanding, unless I am wearing a uniform, it is clear to all that I am the one who has chosen my clothing. And, whether I like or not, this public display of personal preference automatically gives others information about me. Furthermore, if there is a major gap between what I am wearing and my true

1   *Berachot* 20a.

identity, it creates an often humorous cognitive dissonance. We are struck by the contrast between the wearer and the worn when a person wears clothes that are several sizes too large or too small, when an elderly person wears clothing associated with youth, or when a poor person wears very expensive clothing. For better or worse, we expect clothing to accurately reflect the identity of the wearer.

Wealth, size, age, gender and nationality are only the most obvious features of our identities that can be expressed through our clothing. On a more profound level, the subtle variables of our identities such as our interests, personalities, skills, social milieu and experiences can all have expression in the clothes we wear. Of course, human identity is more complex than can ever be completely portrayed by clothing. At the same time, it is amazing how much information can actually be culled by carefully observing a person's clothing. Awareness of this can make us more than a little self-conscious!

In our own times, the issue has become even more acute. The emphasis placed on individual expression and the proliferation of the fashion industry has made us more aware than ever that we can present ourselves in an almost endless combination of "fashion *statements*." It goes without saying that our choice of clothing is somewhat determined by budgetary, aesthetic and other considerations, but arguably foremost on our minds is the statement we will be making. Given the tremendous choice of clothing that exists on the market today, we can spend an inordinate amount of time in a state of confusion, trying to properly, if usually subconsciously, craft the message we believe our clothing should make and then identifying just the right items that will make it. As a result, the Torah's guidance in this increasingly overwhelming task is of particular importance.

Clothing and Character Development

One of the most interesting aspects of humanity is the capacity of the individual for change. This can make a person's awareness of his own developing identity rather elusive – as soon as he comes to understand himself, he has already become someone else. That being the case, knowing oneself and one's essence is no simple matter.

Personal development is not a uniform process. Some experience personal development throughout their lives, whereas others only truly experience it during specific developmental stages. In pre-modern times especially, forming an identity was a relatively uncomplicated and predictable process. Yet most of the major personalities in the Torah, in spite of their pre-modernity, exhibit *dramatic* personal development. When we read about them, we find unusual transformative experiences and challenges repeatedly throughout their lives that cause their identities to change. Indeed, that is one of the major reasons they are so interesting and have such transcendent appeal.

As with anyone else, when Biblical characters change, their clothing frequently does as well. In fact, change of clothing often serves as a device through which the Biblical narrative signals an initiation or confirmation of such a change of identity. To cite an example central to this chapter, Aharon and his children do not become "Kohanim" and cannot officiate as such until they first put on the clothes of their new status.

Nor is it just in the Bible that a change of clothes can indicate a transformation of identity. The most obvious and universal use of clothing to represent such a transformation is at the coronation of a king. Regal garments are axiomatically reserved for a king, and it is only when he dons them that he formally assumes his position. Similarly, a wedding dress is seen as an important element of the ceremony that moves a woman from singlehood to married life. Were such a dress not considered essential to the ceremony, almost everyone would consider it outlandish to wear such a garment, and extravagant to acquire one for just a few hours.

In the previous examples, formal ritual or social conventions dictate that a person wears certain clothing before entering into a new status. More nuanced is the situation wherein a person has to decide for himself whether his identity has changed enough to require the wearing of new clothes. In our own religious culture, a rabbi or rosh yeshiva must decide if and when to don the clothing that is associated with the great rabbis of the past. Since there is no set, prescribed time when such a rabbi will need to acquire these clothes, many will not recognize the elevated status of such a rabbi until he puts on the garments they feel this status requires.

But whether a change of clothing is dictated by convention or by individual self-assessment, it cannot but engender a certain amount of hesitation by the thoughtful wearer. For example, the reflective king will wonder whether he is really fit for his clothes.[2] He will think, "Now that people see me in these new clothes, I will be perceived differently than in the past – does this new outward look accurately reflect my inner development?" In other words, the clothing we wear is not only something that speaks to others about how we see ourselves but it often speaks back to us about who we feel we should be. To be sure, this gives the notion of growing into clothes a completely new meaning.

While in everyday life the symbolism of putting on new clothes is fairly one-dimensional, the Bible rarely limits itself to a monochromatic message. As we shall see, how these clothes are received, what they are made of and how they are seen by others, along with several other variables, all play into the Biblical vision of how to look at new clothes. Let us now turn our attention to the very first new clothes, clothes that would set the tone for everything else that followed.

Changes of Clothing

Though Man is born without clothing, the Torah tells us that his first sin differentiated him from the other creatures around him and made him feel a need to cover himself. Once he felt this need, it led to two different outcomes: First *man* clothes himself by sewing together fig leaves.[3] A bit later, Adam strangely tells God that he is still naked.[4] *God* then responds by clothing him anew in what the Torah describes as "skin-clothes."[5] On the surface, the second set of clothes would seem redundant, since Adam's claim that he was still naked was

---

2   One is reminded of Arthur Green's treatment of Rebbe Nachman's hesitations in assuming the position of Chassidic rebbe in *Tormented Master* (Woodstock, Vermont: Jewish Lights, 1992), especially pp. 40–48.

3   *Bereshit* 3:7.

4   Ibid., 3:10. Several commentators note this peculiarity. See, for example, R. Moshe Alshich and Abarbanel on *Bereshit* 3:10.

5   Ibid., 3:21. Described as *kotnot ohr,* or "skin-suits," it is not clear whether this means that they were made from some type of leather (i.e., suits made from skins) or whether they were simply "suits for the skin."

simply untrue. To leave it at that, however, would give us merely a superficial understanding of the event. Based on our experience with the Biblical text's sophistication and nuance, we know that we have to look further to understand what the Torah is trying to express.

As we try to understand this passage, what strikes us is that the initial set of garments clearly represents man's first attempts to clothe himself. Moreover, their being replaced means that they must have been lacking something. Man tried to meet his own needs, but somehow he was still so "naked" that he felt a need to hide. This first attempt was somehow off the mark.

But what was missing? And what need did the fig leaves try to meet? If they were meant to cover those parts of the body that were understood to be private, what was wrong with them? Did they not accomplish that task adequately? And if not, why had Adam and Chava not sought more leaves or other clothing material? The answer to these questions may become clearer after we look at other examples of how Biblical personalities, when left to their own devices, use and misuse clothing in search of personal identity.

We will start by looking at the final grand narrative in *Bereshit* – the story of Ya'akov and his children. A careful reading of this narrative will show that the theme of clothing keeps reappearing. We should not forget that it is clothing that sets this entire narrative into motion. As expressed by the rabbis, "A couple coins' worth of cloth led to the fateful exile of the Jews in Egypt":[6] the gift of clothing bestowed by Ya'akov on Yosef (and subsequently returned to Ya'akov by Yehudah and the other brothers) was the catalyst of the brothers' discord. But that is not the end of it. As we shall see, both of Ya'akov's two most prominent children, Yehudah and Yosef, encounter several clothing-related events that force them to come to a more profound understanding of clothing – what it should, and should not, be.

We will start our exploration by looking at Yehudah's experiences. Specifically, we will be focusing on someone who seemed to understand clothing far better than anyone in Ya'akov's family, Yehudah's daughter-in-law-cum-wife, Tamar. We will first see how she enlightened Yehudah in this regard and only at that point will we go back to Yosef and see how his clothing becomes

6 *Shabbat* 10b.

the vehicle through which all the brothers evolve in their understanding of clothing.

The Rabbinic Reading of Tamar

The Tamar narrative[7] is one of the more elusive in the Torah. The simple narrative tells us that Tamar married Yehudah's oldest son and after he dies in shadowy circumstances, his second one. After the death of this son, Yehudah promises his third son to her, while sending her away. Since it appears that Yehudah is not keeping his promise, Tamar dresses up as a harlot, waylays Yehudah, and becomes pregnant by him. Not realizing that the child is his, Yehudah sentences her to death.[8] For her part, Tamar subtly lets Yehudah know how she became pregnant, at which point Yehudah declares her to be more righteous than he and rescinds her sentence. This is the simple story, but a more careful reading makes this narrative as rich as it is unusual. The rabbis looked at the events and composed a portrait of Tamar markedly different from what would be drawn if each textual issue were examined in isolation.

The first problem the rabbis confront concerns the place where Tamar became pregnant. *Petach Einayim* is ostensibly merely the name of a place or a description of a place (meaning either crossroads[9] or the entrance to two springs[10]). The rabbis' inquiry is stated in the Midrash, which essentially asks, "How come we've never heard of such a place?" as it is not mentioned anywhere else in Tanakh.[11]

The Talmud has an additional question: why would Tamar's covering her face make Yehudah believe she was a harlot, as a simple reading of the text seems to indicate.[12] If anything, covering her face would seem to be a sign of modesty rather than brazenness. Another issue underlying this section is why,

---

7   *Bereshit* 38.
8   Even as the text says that her crime is sexual infidelity, the nature of this infidelity is not clear. See Ramban on *Bereshit* 38:24.
9   See Rashi, Seforno, Rashbam et al. on *Bereshit* 38:14.
10 See Ibn Ezra on *Bereshit* 38:14.
11 *Bereshit Rabba* 85:7.
12 *Sotah* 10b.

veil or not, Yehudah doesn't recognize his own daughter-in-law in apparent broad daylight. There are possible local answers to these questions,[13] but the Talmud skips over them and instead looks at all the issues together and in context.

The rabbis suggest that *Petach Einayim* is really not a place name at all, but rather a phrase hinting at the type of heroic quest that Tamar had embarked upon. They explain that she had gone to an entrance (*petach*) "that all eyes (*einayim*) would look to" – i.e., the door of Avraham's tent[14] – and surmise that the most likely reason Tamar would go to such a place would be to infuse herself with the spiritual strength needed to proceed with her plan to marry Yehudah.[15] The rabbis interpret Tamar's covering her face in a similarly positive fashion: in fact, the covering didn't take place at the same time as this encounter.[16] Instead, it occurred earlier when she was married to his sons, each time Yehudah was present. Since she always covered her face *then*, he was not familiar enough with her appearance to recognize her *now*.

Thus, the rabbis explain both why a prostitute would cover her face (she wouldn't – Tamar had not covered her face when dressing as a harlot but only earlier), and why Yehudah didn't recognize his first two sons' wife (she had covered her face in his presence all the time that she was married to them). More broadly, the rabbis create a picture of Tamar's activities that better fits in with her virtuous behavior at the end of the story. In seeking a more global understanding of the Tamar narrative, the rabbis were able to see her as a heroine even in her most questionable activities. Granted, this doesn't explain her

13 See, for example, Rabbeinu Bachya on *Bereshit* 38:15, who suggests that it was the way of prostitutes to cover their faces so that they would not be recognized (in the same way as a thief would cover his face today).

14 *Bereshit Rabba* 85:7. While the question the rabbis ask is meant to illuminate the simple understanding of the text, the answer they give is admittedly quite conjectural, indicating the difficulty of finding a more grounded resolution to this issue. Although, they were certainly better expositors of the text than we, we will nonetheless suggest a different answer later in this section.

15 The text doesn't clearly inform us whether marrying Yehudah was indeed her plan. Whatever the reason for her confronting him, it was certainly connected to her being mistreated by him. Challenging someone who is shown later to have the power over her life and death is certainly something for which she would require courage.

16 *Sotah* 10b.

unconventional strategy,[17] but it does frame it in such a way as to minimally require withholding judgment.[18]

The meta-understanding of the narrative outlined above may have been influenced by various subliminal clues in the text which the rabbis did not even articulate, but which, nonetheless, led them to their perspective. We will now look for these clues in order to further illuminate our understanding of Tamar.

Tamar's Clothes

In line with the main topic of this chapter, clothing seems to take on unusual import in the story of Tamar – especially in the discussion of Tamar's meeting with Yehudah at *Petach Einayim*. When the Torah goes into such great detail, telling us that she took off one set of clothing for another and then that she removed that clothing and put the first set back on,[19] it is clearly inviting us to understand the relationship between Tamar and her clothes.

Both the clothes that are identified as "her widow's clothes" and those that can be understood to be harlot's clothes[20] are, like a *uniform*, expressly meant to show an important aspect of Tamar's identity. Yet in actuality, both sets of clothing were essentially only *costumes* – clothing explicitly designed to portray a false identity. She is neither widow (in the sense that a young, childless woman doesn't permanently become a mourner for her first husband) nor prostitute.

It is perhaps for this reason that Tamar so easily changes one set of garments for the other and then back again; she is well aware that her true essence

17 As mentioned in note 15 above, the Biblical text leaves open many questions regarding Tamar's motivations and the strategy she was planning to use when she confronted Yehudah. As such, it is not clear whether she had planned the questionable behavior at the outset or only hastily improvised it due to the unforeseen reaction of Yehudah. Seforno is of the opinion that Tamar expected Yehudah to recognize her, which would have allowed her to tell him her grievance. See also Abarbanel.

18 This helps us appreciate the commentaries that hold that Tamar's decision was the result of some sort of *ruach hakodesh* (holy intuition). See, for example, Ohr ha-Chaim on *Bereshit* 38:14.

19 *Bereshit* 38:14, 19.

20 In line with the approach of Rabbeinu Bachya. See note 13, above.

lies beneath what she chooses to wear. If clothing were to truly define who we are, we would expect it to literally "stick to our flesh." That is to say, it would be as inseparable from us as any other intrinsic part of ourselves. But this is not the case: as illustrated by Tamar, a person is free to dress up as a pious mourner one minute and as a shameless prostitute the next. Indeed, we will soon see that the reason the young Yosef's clothes do seem to stick to his flesh is precisely because he does not understand what Tamar teaches us – that since clothes may be taken on and off at will, we should not expect them to determine who we are.

And it is not just Yosef who wants to identify people via their clothes. That Yehudah also has such a penchant comes out clearly in his relationship with Tamar. In fact, until the end of the story Yehudah *completely* identifies Tamar with what she wears at any given time. Truth be told, his inability to properly recognize her actually goes beyond her clothing. Several commentators[21] suggest that when Yehudah originally sends Tamar away, it is because he misjudges her, holding her accountable for the death of his two older sons. Nonetheless, his initial misperception seems to be greatly amplified further on in the narrative, when he takes Tamar to be a prostitute simply because she is dressed as such. At that point, his impressions of Tamar seem completely limited to the superficial, to what "meets the *eye*."

The story continues to unfold into one long string of events that could be described as a type of hide-and-seek, where Yehudah sends his friend to look for someone who doesn't exist (the prostitute) – only to be confronted by someone else (Tamar) who actually was the person for whom he was searching all along (the woman who will be the mother of his children and of the Davidic lineage). Yehudah's inability to see the authentic is further driven home when Tamar tells him to "*recognize*" the identity of the items that she had received as surety from him.[22] The Torah tells us that he recognizes, but it doesn't give us the subject of his recognition ("Yehudah recognized and said"[23]). Based on

---

21 See, for example, Rashi on *Bereshit* 38:11, based on *Bereshit Rabba* 85:5.
22 One of the items that comprised the surety was a garment that Yehudah had probably needed to take off. Maybe here too, Tamar was trying to drive home the idea that clothing is contingent and not part of a person's essence.
23 *Bereshit* 38:26.

this textual anomaly, we can suggest that he recognized more than the objects that belonged to him. Yehudah finally "sees": Not only does he now recognize that the woman who appeared to be (i.e., wore the clothes of) a prostitute was really Tamar, he also recognizes that Tamar was a spiritual giant ("*tzadka mimeni*"[24]) and certainly could not have been at fault for the death of his sons, as he might have previously thought.

Once Yehudah is able to "recognize," the Torah tells us that he came to "know" Tamar – significantly in a situation that is devoid of clothing.[25] (Granted, this is actually the second time that the two had conjugal relations, but the circumstances of the first encounter were such that no true recognition was possible.) To follow the key verbs in the narrative, Yehudah first *sees* but doesn't *know* Tamar, then he *searches* but cannot *find* her, and finally he is led to *re-cognize*, which leads him to ultimately *know* her and not just her appearance.

At this point, it seems almost impossible not to notice another allusion created by the place where Tamar met Yehudah. There could be no more apt description of what Tamar was trying to orchestrate than *Petach Einayim*, an "opening of the eyes." At *Petach Einayim*, she initiates the process that opens Yehudah's eyes to her essence as well as to the understanding that "clothes don't make the (wo)man."

Yehudah and Yosef

The rabbis also notice that Yehudah's recognition of his own belongings[26] is couched in the same language that the brothers used in showing Yosef's bloodied clothing to their father, Ya'akov.[27] This additional

---

24 Ibid.
25 Whether the final words of *Bereshit* 38:26 are telling us that Tamar and Yehudah continued to live conjugally or ceased to do so is actually a matter of great debate. We have followed the approach of the rabbis in tractate *Sotah*, who posit the former. (See *Torah Temimah* ad loc., note 34, who lends support to this reading and also Netziv ad loc., who suggests a third understanding of the verse.)
26 *Bereshit* 38:26.
27 Ibid., 37:32.

observation sets up a powerful contrast between the two episodes.[28]

Earlier, when Yehudah had asked his father to "recognize" Yosef's tunic, it was still a superficial recognition that he was talking about – of Yosef via his clothing. For when Yehudah engineered the sale of Yosef, he was seeking to sell the bearer of the regal tunic made by, and now returned to, Ya'akov. It does not appear that Yehudah made any effort to understand Ya'akov's love for the Yosef who lay underneath the garment – the Yosef who would show so much strength of character and sensitivity later on.[29] Thus, it is no coincidence that directly after that episode, we see Tamar teaching Yehudah that the definition of a person via his or her clothing is problematic: he ends up depending on the image the other person projects through the latter's outer appearance. Even assuming that a person is trying to project himself honestly, that image is only as accurate as the person is self-aware. Additionally, even an honest self-portrait may represent an ambition and not a current reality.

(The context of Yehudah's new recognition is a story of a major personal turnaround, wherein Yehudah shows tremendous change.[30] It is a story that begins with a forebodingly dark descent and ends with a moral and physical rebirth, which sets the stage for Yehudah to gradually become the leader of his brothers.[31] If we are aware of this context, we almost expect the second recognition to be a *tikkun*, a correction, of the first.)

Once Yehudah has learned about the unreliability of clothing from Tamar, he will know not to judge the Egyptian viceroy by his superficially intimidating clothing, but by what he can decipher from his words and actions. Moreover, he will also be in a better position to reevaluate whether the younger, osten-

---

28 *Bereshit Rabba* 85:11.

29 A further allusion that the brothers are relying too heavily on Yosef's clothing is the response of the two individuals that disagree with the brothers' assessment of Yosef – when first Reuven and then Ya'akov hear about what has happened to Yosef, they both tear their *clothes*. We will take up this idea again later in the chapter.

30 See Zvi Grumet, "Patriarch and King – Two Models of Repentance," in the soon-to-be-published *Ohr Chadash: Writings from the Beit Midrash of Avraham Avinu* (Jerusalem: David Cardozo Academy).

31 For more on the process of his rise to leadership, see *Redeeming Relevance in Genesis*, Chapter 6.

sibly obnoxious Yosef really deserved the fate that the brothers meted out to him in the first place.

It is only after the episode with Tamar[32] that Yehudah is able to return to Yosef and begin the process of family reconciliation in Egypt. Shaky though it may have been, the reuniting of the brothers could not have come about until Yehudah was able to look beyond Yosef's clothing – which, ironically, had become only more alienating once he became the viceroy of Egypt. For his present garments were no longer the symbol of favoritism of a common beneficent father. Instead, they represented semi-despotic authority and allegiance to a nation that would become Israel's nemesis.[33]

Yosef's Clothes

If the theme of clothing in the Tamar narrative were not clear enough, it becomes even clearer from its blatant placement in the middle of the Yosef story.[34] In the latter story, too, which transpires both immediately before and immediately after the account of Yehudah and Tamar, we see the text's taking special interest in Yosef's interaction with clothing.

Even as both stories deal with putting on and taking off distinctive clothing, the ways that Yosef and Tamar relate to their clothes are markedly different – so much so that Yosef can be seen as Tamar's alter ego. If Tamar feels that she can fool *others* by wearing certain clothes, it appears that the young Yosef fools *himself*, thinking that his clothing automatically defines his true identity.

In this regard, it is significant that Yosef does not have his dreams about

32 Some commentators suggest that this narrative occurred before the sale of Yosef (most notably, Ibn Ezra, on *Bereshit* 38:1). Such a suggestion may paradoxically strengthen our contention, that Yehudah's interaction with Tamar would be a prerequisite to his reevaluation of Yosef, in the sense that the Torah must feel very strongly about a *conceptual* sequence in order to upset the chronology. According to this chronology, we may say that the lesson Yehudah learned from Tamar did not completely sink in until the Yosef story further unfolded. To simplify matters, however, here we will assume that the major encounter of Yehudah and Tamar took place after the sale of Yosef.

33 See Chapter 1.

34 This unusual placement is noted by Rashi, Ibn Ezra, Rabbenu Bachya and others.

domination over his family until after his father gives him the special tunic.[35] It is as if the acquisition of this garment makes him believe, perhaps only somewhat incorrectly, that he has been elected to be the leader of the clan. It is to this perception that his father Ya'akov addresses himself when he rhetorically asks his son, "Am I also to bow down to you?"[36] When he hears this, Yosef is silent.

Jewish tradition understands an interlocutor's silence to generally indicate agreement. In the above case, Yosef's silence indicates agreement with his father that he has overshot the mark. In other words, he accepts his father's rebuke that, at least *for right now*, his newly acquired "breeches were too big for him." At the same time, both Ya'akov and Yosef have a premonition that these clothes (or, more precisely, similar ones given him later by Pharaoh) would one day fit, even if it meant that Yosef would become more powerful than his father even in the latter's lifetime. Hence, though Yosef may well have been stifled by his father's critique, he would still have to travel a long journey before learning the lesson that Tamar had taught Yehudah – that the clothes a person wears are, at best, an imperfect indicator of who they really are.

The Torah shows very clearly that the focus of the brothers' hatred is Yosef's attachment to his tunic (and the identity it represents). It describes the brothers first ripping it off him (presumably tearing it in the process) and then slaughtering a goat, specifically to cover this hated tunic in the blood of death. By taking the tunic away from Yosef as well as by symbolically "killing" it, the brothers were sending the obvious message that Yosef should abandon his identification with the garment. At the same time, and as we will discuss again later, the brothers' desire to differentiate Yosef from his clothing is ambivalent. On the one hand, they feel that he is not their master and that his clothes don't accurately represent him. On the other hand, like Yehudah, they could not see beyond Yosef's self-perception as reflected in his clothes.

Whereas both Yosef and his brothers identified him with his clothes, the Biblical report seems to want to correct this mistake right on the spot. The

35 See Thomas Mann's humorous, fanciful account of the tunic's lineage and Yosef's hunger for it in *Joseph and his Brothers* (New York: Alfred A. Knopf, 1986) pp. 314–23.
36 *Bereshit* 37:10.

brothers only physically separate Yosef from his clothes, while the text indicates a parallel *conceptual* separation. It does so by offering us the otherwise superfluous information that the tunic the brothers took was the one "upon him."[37] Could the Torah not be asking us to note that it was only *upon* him, but not *of* him? In that case, all other perceptions to the contrary notwithstanding, the narrative's objective perspective reports that Yosef's essence actually lies past his clothes. Yet whether we are reading this phrase correctly or not, the rest of the narrative certainly suggests such an idea. We now turn our attention to how this comes out from the developing plot.

Most significant for us in the Yosef story's opening scene is that he has his clothes taken off by *others*.[38] In contrast to his future encounters with clothing as well as in clear contrast to Tamar, Yosef appears unready to take them off himself. Not only that; according to several commentators, the choice of words here indicates that the struggle with Yosef over his tunic was so intense that it required his brothers to rip off all of his other clothes as well.[39] In this way, Yosef was telling his brothers that separating him from his clothing was unthinkable and that the attempt to do so was, in actual fact, tantamount to violating his very essence.

Like his older brother Yehudah, once separated from the rest of his family, Yosef shows serious growth. But as is normally the case with human beings, he does so gradually. The first stage of growth is in Potiphar's house. There, Yosef is still not able to stop himself from taking on a persona dictated by his outer appearance. The Torah tells us that he was of beautiful form and looks,[40] a description usually reserved for women. The rabbis did not miss this allusion and tell us that Yosef groomed himself to an unusual degree in the house of Potiphar.[41] While this behavior may well have been politically or even religiously motivated, it likely made him appear more feminine than the other men around him. And so, in striking contrast to the story of Yehudah and Tamar, it is Potiphar's wife who adopts the traditionally masculine role

37 See Ohr haChayim and Kli Yakar on *Bereshit* 37:23.
38 *Bereshit* 37:23.
39 Op. cit. note 37.
40 *Bereshit* 39:6.
41 *Midrash Tanchuma*, Parashat Vayeshev.

of sexual aggressor (and a tireless one at that), while Yosef finds himself in the customarily feminine position of victim. It is not likely that so unusual a situation was only prompted by the lusting of Potiphar's wife. Rather, it stands to reason that it was also brought about by Yosef as well. Among other things, once Yosef took on a more feminine *appearance*, he may have also felt forced to take on a more feminine role, prompting his female adversary to assume a more assertive stance.

In any case, by the end of his tenure in Potiphar's house, Yosef takes a large step away from his previously fatalistic identification with his outer appearance. Although we cannot be sure, it would make sense that, as the chief domestic officer of the highly placed Potiphar, Yosef would be given some uniform to match his status. As with the tunic he received from his father, such a garment would represent power and prestige. Nonetheless, as opposed to the first garment that he lost to his brothers, when he loses this new one, he *chooses* to lose it. Granted, he does so in desperation in order to escape the clutches of Potiphar's wife, but he leaves it in her hands out of his own volition. Running out of the clothing instead of having it ripped off, means that Yosef now saw more of a separation between himself and his clothing. When he received the special tunic from his father, he saw himself and his clothing as interchangeable and thus could not fathom being without them – until they were forcibly removed. Since then, Yosef grows to the point that he is willing to see some room for separation from his clothes, if admittedly only under duress.

If his further encounters with clothing are an indication – and it would seem that they are – Yosef's comportment with Potiphar's wife still represents only an in-between stage and not the final step in his growth. But if he is no longer stripped of his clothing, neither is he the one who *initiates* its separation from him. For that we need to wait until the next stage of his life.

When Yosef gets out of jail to have an audience with the Egyptian king, he is finally able to be freer with his clothing. In that scene,[42] as well as soon afterward when he is appointed viceroy,[43] the Torah gets unusually interested in the details of Yosef's getting dressed. Especially in the first case, is it not

---

42 *Bereshit* 41:14.
43 Ibid., verse 42.

obvious that one would need to dress up before seeing a king? This reminds us of the same unusual interest the Torah showed in Tamar's getting dressed. The Torah's focus on these particular details shows us that Yosef's new set of garments constitutes another link in the maturing of his attitude toward clothing. The Torah is making the point that Yosef does not cling to his immediate past identity of head prisoner, as he had once clung to other previous identities. Now, when the situation calls for it, he simply takes off his clothes by himself. Likewise, he can readily put on the next set of clothing as needed: he can wear the clothes of a free man, even if he is still a servant.

In brief, when he comes out of jail, Yosef is finally willing to admit that he is not defined by his clothing. Just as Tamar had originally known that one can wear costumes and not be determined by them, now Yosef also comes around to this realization. As a result, the Torah will no longer speak about his clothing being ripped off.

We have further indication of Yosef's later spiritual growth as it relates to his attitude toward clothing in the unusual word choice regarding the clothing around him. First, when he changes his garments to appear in front of Pharaoh,[44] and then when he gives his brothers clothing before returning to Canaan to bring back their father,[45] the Torah uses terms derived from the Hebrew root *chalaf*, to change or substitute (*vayechalef, chalifot simla'ot*). We almost never see *vayechalef* anywhere else in the entire Bible[46] and the term *chalifot* is not found anywhere else in the Torah – though it is employed in the early prophets. In the context of what we have already learned about Yosef's clothes, this is a superbly purposeful word choice: the Torah is telling us that Yosef now sees clothing as something that can be *changed* at will without its changing the essence of the person it covers. So much is Yosef aware of this that he is now even in a position to convey this message to his brothers. (In doing so, he again parallels Tamar, who conveys the same message to Yehudah.)

◆ ◆ ◆

44 Ibid., verse 14.
45 Ibid., 45:22.
46 The two exceptions are in *Bereshit* 35:2 and in *Tehillim* 102:27.

As in the earlier narrative of Yehudah and Tamar, the Midrash formulates the point of resolution in this story as a situation where Yosef is without clothing altogether. The Torah tells us that the brothers were taken aback when Yosef revealed himself as their long lost brother. The Midrash, however, wonders what convinced them to believe that this man, who had appeared so foreign to them during all this time, was really Yosef. The answer given is that Yosef *removed his clothing* to show the brothers his circumcision.[47] If admittedly speculative, this midrash helps us complete the parallel to Tamar, who, as mentioned earlier, is only completely known for who she is when she is unclothed as well. Thus, like Tamar, Yosef has transformed himself to the point where he is able to transmit the truth of his identity, but significantly only when he has removed his clothes.

Not coincidentally, the stages in Yosef's understanding parallel the stages in his political career. When Yosef saw himself as inextricably connected to what his regal clothing represented, it was torn away from him by force and he was exiled – a punishment traditionally reserved for the most threatening prisoners. In his next stage at the house of Potiphar, Yosef is punished in a less extreme fashion. That is because even as Yosef's personality was still determined by his clothing, he had at least realized that identity has some flexibility outside of what one wears. That being the case, one may sometimes make the "bold move" of escaping from clothing that, Yosef still believed, generally dictates who one is. When Yosef leaves his garments in the hands of Potiphar's wife, he must have known that, at the very least, he would be demoted from his position as Potiphar's manager. Yet at that point, he had correspondingly become less desperate to hold on to the position of leadership that he felt was linked to his true identity. At this level of understanding, he is perceived as less of a threat than he had been earlier and is only imprisoned, not exiled.

At some point while he was imprisoned, Yosef must have learned to divorce himself from his clothing and, like Tamar, view it as something that may be changed with relative ease. Once he reaches that point and does not feel *compelled* to be the leader – just because Pharaoh gives him a set of leader's clothes – he is able to stay in power in clothing that no one needs to rip off.

47 *Midrash Tanchuma*, Parashat Vayigash.

Not only that, he has come full circle, as now others (i.e., Pharaoh), instead of wanting to take prestigious clothes *off* of him, seek to place such clothes *upon* him.

It essence, the stories of Yehudah and Yosef actually drive home the same point under different circumstances. The lesson that Yehudah must learn about the essence of others, Yosef must learn about himself. Still, common to Yehudah and Yosef is the fact that they do learn and grow from adversity – an adversity that has its origins in their common misunderstanding of clothing.

The Prehistory of Yosef's Clothes

Of course, Yehudah's and Yosef's involvement with clothing does not tell the whole story. Though they, along with Tamar, are this thematic tapestry's central figures, the motif of clothing and its significance is found in the rest of the family as well. To begin with, one cannot help noticing that it is specifically *Ya'akov's* two sons who make similar mistakes regarding the ability of clothing to determine identity. Moreover, inasmuch as all of the brothers implicated in the sale of Yosef judged him by his clothes, we can conclude that the problem with clothing is really endemic to *all* of Ya'akov's children.

Consequently, it is not unreasonable to look for something in Ya'akov's own life experience that would explain his children's ill-fated dependence on what they think is being communicated via clothing. Looking back at Ya'akov's life, his most significant interaction with clothing occurs when his mother tells him to put on Esav's garments in order to impersonate him and receive their father's blessing.[48] At first glance this famous passage would seem to show behavior similar to Tamar's, as Ya'akov is putting on a costume which he knows is at odds with his true identity. If anything, this should make him aware of the inability of clothing to truly identify someone.

---

48 *Bereshit* 27:15–16. That the Torah considers clothing to be significant in the life of Ya'akov himself can be surmised from the fact that it is completely silent about of all of his predecessors' interactions with clothing. The last time we read anything about clothing was with Adam and Chava. In contrast, we have three mentions of clothing with Ya'akov even before the Yosef and Yehudah narratives begin. See also *Bereshit* 27:27 and *Bereshit* 28:20.

But if we look more carefully, we will see that Ya'akov was resistant to such use of clothing. Completely not present is the ease with which Tamar replaces one set of garments with another. Instead, Ya'akov appears to hesitate in fulfilling what his mother construes to be his filial obligation to her. This ambivalence is illustrated by the fact that it is Rivka who actually places the clothes upon him. (More about this later.) Certainly, Ya'akov was old enough to put the clothes on by himself. But in the context of his obvious discomfort with the whole plan, he appears to be far from enamored with this part of his mother's suggestion as well.

Could Ya'akov's ambivalence stem from a sense that clothing cannot be used in the way demanded by his mother? Might he feel that using clothes in an inauthentic manner is no different from using words in an inauthentic manner – in other words, lying? Sure it can be done, but it is base and unethical to do so. Hence, for Ya'akov it is only under duress and in very unusual circumstances that one can wear anything except the clothes he *should* be wearing – i.e., those that portray who he is.

For Ya'akov, clothing is as transparent a form of communication as speech: just as the words we use have an agreed meaning, so too do clothes. Furthermore, our choice of clothing is no less self-aware than our choice of speech. If Ya'akov did not understand clothing as clear, self-aware communication, wearing Esav's clothes would not have presented an ethical dilemma.

It follows that Ya'akov, known in Jewish tradition for his love of truth, would have strongly impressed upon his children his views about not wearing "false" clothing. So strongly, in fact, that they could not imagine a righteous person's essence deviating from that which is communicated by what he wears. And so, when the brothers rip Yosef's clothes off of him, they do so in response to what they see as an arrogant *lie* – Yosef's wearing the mantle of leadership when he is not their leader.

Hence, if Yehudah and Yosef begin their respective journeys with an overly one-sided vision of the function of clothing, it could well be traced back to their father. At the same time, their perspective should not be dismissed completely. In a way, Ya'akov and sons have it right; since clothing does communicate information about ourselves, should we not generally try to wear garments that engage in honest communication? Perhaps. But the moral correctness of this position did not necessarily have to lead to the brothers' attitude toward Yosef.

Until the messianic era clothing, even more than words, cannot simply be taken at face value for at least two major reasons: (1) Clothing is static. As briefly discussed above, a person changes from one moment to the next. A dynamic individual takes on new attitudes and incorporates new life experiences that make him different from when he first acquired any given piece of clothing. In contrast to this, that clothing stays the same. Granted, we can add a sash here or a ribbon there, but there is no way for an individual garment to keep up with the ever-vibrant human personality. (2) Whereas most verbal communication is about relatively objective information outside of ourselves, clothing is almost always about ourselves and resultantly shaped by our imperfect self-knowledge. One doesn't need to be a psychologist to know that a person's self-knowledge is hopelessly subjective, often to the point of being completely flawed. As a result, the idealistic vision of clothing held by Ya'akov and passed on to his sons was bound to lead to problems in the "real world."

Yet there is tremendous value to Ya'akov's perspective even in the here and now. At the end of the day, people *do* communicate about themselves via clothing – no matter how imperfect a vehicle it is. As a result, since people do have reason to analyze what we are wearing, we should strive to be honest in what we wear. Ya'akov teaches us the moral component in choosing clothes that identify us as authentically as possible. From this typically Jewish perspective of heightened sensitivity to our actions, then, choosing what we ourselves wear becomes morally charged. It becomes dangerous, however, when we apply this standard to others. Even if we have to be honest with what we wear, we should generally not look to the clothing of others as being either a correct indicator of their personality or a wanton lie.

It is interesting to note further that Ya'akov and his sons' overly idealistic view of clothing would be corrected primarily by people, outside of the family. (Rivka, who in her disagreement with Ya'akov could be seen as the first to try to correct his view, could, as a foreign-born woman, also fit this category.) As one of the unpleasant realities of the "real world," this may have been something that the Jews would have to learn from those who came from less idealistic cultures.

To fill out our discussion of Yosef and clothing, we cannot help but notice the frequent tearing of clothes that occurs in response to the tragedies surrounding him. Given what we have seen thus far, it is hard not to conclude that this is also part of the tapestry woven into the Yosef narrative. In the context of our understanding, when Reuven, then Ya'akov and then of all the brothers tear their clothes, one senses a semi-prophetic irony at play: their roles in this tragedy all stem from overreliance on the message Yosef was sending out with his clothes. And their response was to tear clothing – the very thing that was getting them into trouble to begin with. Still, as is often the case in life, it appears that they did not fully internalize this connection until much later.

Clothing as a Verb

Given the problematic nature of clothing, it may seem initially surprising that classical Judaism views the act of clothing another as very praiseworthy.[49] Of course, when we think about it further, we could conclude that clothing as a charitable act is viewed independently of its communicative functions. After all, when God gives Adam and Chava clothing, the most important purpose appears to be His taking care of their basic needs. Still, we can't ignore the fact that when God satisfied their requirements of warmth and privacy, He did so with *clothes* and so, simultaneously, gave them a device that would communicate information to themselves and to each other.

To be sure, clothing another person carries multiple meanings. Maybe more than any other act, it is to be found in the intersection of primal needs and social interaction. The convergence of these worlds highlights the fascinating dichotomy of human existence in general – between the natural existence that we ultimately have in common with animals and human artifice that can allow us to reach great heights or, alternatively, stoop to the depths. Be that as it may, it will be instructive to see the Torah's treatment of clothing others in the various narratives where it takes place.

49 Jewish tradition, lists "clothing the naked" as one of the classical ways of emulating God's kindness. See *Sotah* 14a.

It should immediately be noted that the placing of clothes on someone occurs only at a very few critical junctures in the Torah. The first time is when God clothes Adam and Chava. The only other time that *God* is manifestly involved in dressing someone is when He tells Moshe to place the (Divinely designed) priestly garments on Aharon and his sons. The connection between these two scenes was not lost on the rabbis – several midrashim suggest that the clothes God gave Adam and Chava were, in fact, the priestly robes themselves.[50] This idea is bolstered by one of the major medieval commentators, Rabbenu Bachya,[51] who brings to our attention that the exact phrasing "*vayalbishem*" (*he* dressed *them*), appears only in these two stories. Later, we will see that these narratives have more in common than just these similarities. But before we do so, we should put them in the context of other similar narratives.

In fact, we read of only two other cases in which the Torah describes people clothing others.[52] At this point, we are already familiar with both of them: when Rivka places Esav's clothes on Ya'akov[53] and when Pharaoh places royal

50 See *Bemidbar Rabba* 4:8 and *Tanchuma Yashan*, Toledot 12.

51 On *Bereshit* 3:21, comparing this verse to *Vaykira* 8:13. This usage of the *hiph'il* (causative/plural) verb appears only in these two places, since it is the only time that we see one figure clothing more than one other character.

52 Although there are only two such stories in the Torah, there are a few more in the rest of the Tanakh. For example, when King Shaul uses his own armor to cover David (*I Shmuel* 17:38) and when God tells Yeshayahu that He will dress Elyakim ben Chilkiyahu (*Yeshayahu* 22:21.) In general, these stories follow the outline we will describe, i.e., the benevolence of someone who covers another with new and better clothes. (The story of Haman's clothing Mordechai in the book of *Esther* is typical of the irony of that book, wherein Haman plays the role of the, in this case reluctant, benefactor who imitates God.)

53 It is perhaps not surprising that another midrash identifies this cloak too with the one given by God to Adam (See R. M. Kasher's *Torah Shelemah*, *Bereshit* 3:21, note 184), while still another identifies it with the clothing of the Kohen Gadol (see *Talmud Yerushalmi*, *Megila* 1:12). It appears that there is even a Midrashic tradition that combines both of these opinions, identifying the clothing of Esav with both the *bigdei kehuna* and Adam's clothing; see *Torah Shelemah*, *Bereshit* 27:15, note 66. However, Esav's clothing is more commonly associated with a *different conception* of the first clothes given to Adam, according to which the clothes have less to do with the bearer's relationship with God (i.e., *kehuna*) than they do with his dominion over the animals (See *Yalkut Shimoni*, *Bereshit* 62 and *Bereshit Rabba* 65:16). Though one could combine both themes, saying that the garments that gave

garments on Yosef. In both cases, God is notably absent. Still, as with the Divine clothing of Adam and Chava and as with the priestly robes, we witness a benevolent figure granting advantage through an active bestowal of clothing. Hence, even if God is not directly involved, there is an emulation of God's dressing of man.

If we look more carefully at these stories, we will notice that the job of clothing someone else is more complicated than first meets the eye. If it is obvious that clothes must "fit the man" physically, it should not be forgotten that, at least ideally, clothes must fit the man on the highly nuanced, communicative level as well.

Thus, emulating God in this regard requires the wisdom to know what clothes are needed by the one whom we are trying to clothe. In the Bible, this translates into assigning a role about which the giver of the garments has greater insight than the receiver.

Accordingly, Rivka felt it was up to her alone to clothe her son. When she placed Esav's special clothing on Ya'akov, she was giving him the garments of the firstborn so he would receive the blessing that was reserved for Yitzchak's eldest child. With the change of clothing, she was effectively acting out a decision *she* had made about Ya'akov's identity: that birth order notwithstanding, he was truly the firstborn. It should be clear that this was not something with which Ya'akov agreed. On the contrary, Ya'akov's hesitation about complying with his mother's plan showed that he remained ambivalent, at best, about the role that Rivka was thrusting upon him. But this had no impact on his mother. To Rivka, Ya'akov's unwillingness to seek out these garments only meant that he did not truly understand himself. Since she did, it was up to her to provide him with the clothing that he really needed, whether he knew it or not.

In Yosef's case, it was Pharaoh who decided his identity. Granted, Yosef could not dress himself up as the viceroy without the Egyptian king's consent,

---

dominion over animals were also those of the sacrificial rite, there don't appear to be any midrashim that do so. Since the latter association of Esav's clothes with Adam's "animal clothes," is more common, we may conclude that the connection between Esav's clothing and the *bigdei kehuna* remains tenuous, whereas the connection between Adam's garments and the *bigdei kehuna* is more grounded in the Biblical text and its accompanying interpretive tradition.

but it was likely more than this that stopped him from demanding the clothing of Egyptian royalty. As a Jew, the role of Egyptian viceroy would also bring with it the Jew-in-exile's classical problem of dual loyalty. In contrast to Yosef's probable hesitation, Pharaoh was convinced that *he* understood Yosef better and could tell him who he really was ("There is no one as clever and wise as you"[54]). His opinion of Yosef is further ratified by the new Egyptian name he gives him.[55] Could there be any better way for one to tell another person that he understands him better than the latter understands himself? In the same way that Rivka told Ya'akov, "You are truly the firstborn even though you were born second," Pharaoh is telling Yosef, "You are now an Egyptian lord even though you were born a Jew."

That someone else should be more aware of our identities than we ourselves are should not come as a complete surprise. Indeed, when Yehudah and Yosef finally understand the problematic nature of clothing, they both come to realize that even when a person is not trying to deceive someone else, the former may still unwittingly be sending off incorrect messages about his own identity – because identity is so complex. Hence a person is not always the best judge of what he should be wearing. Since an insightful second party can have a better sense of another's identity than he himself has, the Bible presents us with scenes of such people deciding how to clothe others. As we shall see, however, no matter how wise, they cannot completely emulate God. To put it back into appropriate metaphor, the clothing they prescribe will never completely fit. Consequently, Rivka's and Pharaoh's benevolent intentions notwithstanding, their emulation of God remains incomplete.

Rivka was right but she was also wrong. She was right because the blessing that she sought for Ya'akov was one whose author, Yitzchak, eventually also agreed should go to him.[56] Still, this was not accomplished without engendering Esav's ire and without setting into motion a tragic, if perhaps necessary,[57]

---

54 *Bereshit* 41:39.
55 See *Redeeming Relevance in Genesis* pp. 87–88, concerning the significance of a name change in the Bible. See also *Rosh Hashanah* 16b and Maharal in *Chiddushei Aggadot*.
56 See *Bereshit* 27:33–41.
57 See Chapter 3.

personal exile that would seriously compromise the formation of Ya'akov's own family.[58]

Maybe even more obvious than the oversights of Rivka are those of Pharaoh. The involuntary Jewish immigrant to Egypt that Pharaoh would raise up could indeed help his new homeland. At the same time, Yosef would also remain distinct. He would never become the complete Egyptian that Pharaoh thought he would become. He may have married an Egyptian priest's daughter and been given an Egyptian name, but he would always be a Jew. This is symbolized most clearly when he requests in the strongest of terms that his bones be taken out of Egypt when the Jews would eventually leave the country.[59] Given the fact that Pharaoh is only partially correct in his assessment of Yosef, it should come as no surprise that when Yosef does assume the identity given him by Pharaoh, it complicates matters. For one thing, it allows him to plot some sort of intrigue against his brothers, who would not be able to recognize him in the guise of the "Egyptian man" (as he is described by them).[60] But besides the problem it creates for Yosef's brothers, it also created a problem for the Jews as a whole. Pharaoh's attempt to determine Yosef's identity puts a Jew in the national spotlight, something which commonly leads to judging the rest of the Jewish nation according to that Jew's popularity or unpopularity. Indeed, it is quite possibly Yosef's austere economic policies that would plant the seeds for the Jews' oppression in Egypt after his death.

58 In the sense that the squabbles that ensued among Ya'akov's wives and subsequently among his children were caused by his unplanned marriage to Leah, which was in turn caused by his weak status and power as a stranger in Lavan's home. (See also Chapter 3.)

59 *Bereshit* 50:25.

60 See Chapter 6 of *Redeeming Relevance in Genesis* for a discussion of Yosef's foreignness in the eyes of his brothers. As discussed there, Yosef was truly more capable of being Egyptian than they. Pharaoh may well have sensed this when he made the decision to "clothe" Yosef in Egyptian garb.

Adam Revisited

We are now in a better position to understand the nakedness felt by Adam and Chava even after they had designed their own clothes.[61] The stories just discussed suggest the critical distinction between these very first clothes and those which were given them by God. Since a human being can never completely understand someone's identity, the clothing he chooses for himself or for others will never completely "fit." The only One Who can fit us with perfect clothing is God Himself.

Hence, when Adam and Chava designed their own clothes, they may have been ideally suited to their physical needs at the time, but they could not be ideally suited to their identities. For this, God had to enter the scene. Indeed, the "nakedness" they felt even after they had made themselves garments was not a nakedness of being without clothes; it was the nakedness of not having *true* clothes – clothes that would authentically reflect their identities. It could be that this is why the Midrash says that the meaning of these *kotnot ohr*, "skin-suits," was that God made clothes that really did "stick to their skins."[62]

Right at the beginning of creation, then, man is presented with the real and the ideal. The first set of clothes that man designed for himself would be the real clothes of our existence, which communicate in an imperfect way. The Divine second set of clothes, which communicate perfectly, were the ideal that Ya'akov and his sons mistakenly thought already existed when they attached so much significance to Yosef's tunic. This distinction of human clothing versus Divine clothing is not only symbolized by who it is that designs the respective sets of clothing, it is also symbolized by who is doing the dressing. After all, God did not have to dress Adam and Chava. He could have simply given them the new garments to put on themselves. Presumably, this too carries its own significance.

In this regard, the story of Yosef aids our understanding once again. On some level, it serves as a point of transition between the problematic human use of clothing and its pristine function as endowed by God. When Yosef gets

---

61 See notes 3–5 and their associative text, above.
62 *Bereshit Rabba* 20:12.

his special clothing from Ya'akov, his father *doesn't place it upon him*. At that point Yosef still felt that he could understand who he was, based on what he wore. That he would put on the garments himself shows us that he was the one who decided whether he would wear it or not. It is only when Yosef understands that human clothing cannot properly reflect one's identity that he has new clothes *placed upon him*, evoking – albeit imperfectly – the Divine placement of clothing that we find at man's creation. Being clothed by someone else symbolizes an individual's acceptance of his inability to completely understand himself. Whether he is clothed by God or by another person, when someone accepts his own inability to completely know himself, he realizes where he stands in relation to perfection – where he stands in front of God.

This insight notwithstanding, the clothing of Adam has even more fundamental undertones. When man is sent into the world as a result of his sin, he immediately becomes aware of the world's imperfection. At the same time, according to Jewish tradition, bringing the world back to a state of pre-sin pristine harmony, of *tikkun*, stands at the center of man's historical challenge. This presents an obvious problem; namely, how can we strive for a perfection of which we, as mortals in an imperfect world, are not experientially aware?[63] Man cannot know much about the perfection that he is trying to create, since he has never really seen it.

In order to give man a model to guide his efforts towards *tikkun* of the human world, there is a need for him to experience what perfect communication could be. This is the clothing that God gave Adam, and which, according to one tradition, was passed down from generation to generation.[64]

Adam's Clothes and Aharon's Clothes

As mentioned, the Torah gives us two scenarios where God is the One Who dictates the clothing that should be worn. So far, we have looked at the first

---

63 It might be said that the natural world works perfectly. Even were we to grant such a position, it certainly cannot be said that the world of human interaction and communication could claim any type of perfection.

64 See note 53, above.

scenario at the very beginning of the Torah. Let us now look at the second scenario – the dressing of Aharon and his sons.

It should be made clear that there was no obvious need for the institution of priestly garments altogether. The association of special clothing with leadership is far from a foregone conclusion, not being required of Moshe or Aharon before the creation of the Mishkan (Tabernacle). Neither are special garments obviously required for the priestly rites. Regarding the firstborn, who offered sacrifices before being replaced by the Kohanim, [65] we have no indication that they wore special clothing for this purpose.[66] Neither is it obvious that the special ritual clothing should be dedicated by having them *placed* on Aharon – why couldn't he dress himself?[67]

These questions may fall away if, as per the midrashim mentioned earlier, the placing of Aharon's and his sons' clothing was, in fact, modeled on God's dressing of Adam and Chava: In the very first placement of clothing, God knew exactly what His creations needed. No doubt here too, God dictated the ideal clothing for the practitioners of the Temple service. Also like Adam and Chava, who were made to realize that perfect clothing can come only from God, the point that even the greatest of the Kohanim would not know how to choose clothes for himself could best be expressed by putting Aharon's clothes upon him.

Granted, there are some important differences between the two scenarios. That here God works through Moshe as opposed to placing the clothes directly on Aharon is only the most obvious. Still, these differences, which may

---

65 See *Shemot* 24:5 and *Bemidbar* 3:45.

66 See *Bemidbar Rabba* 4:8, which claims otherwise. Still, it would be difficult to find any textual basis for the notion that the firstborn wore priestly robes. Moreover, this is based on the idea that the garments of Adam and Chava were priestly garments, which, even in the world of Midrash, is a point of contention. See note 53, above.

67 An interesting answer to this question is suggested by the rabbinic reading of *Vayikra* 9:7, wherein God's command that Moshe *bring* Aharon close to the ritual service is understood to mean that Aharon did not feel fit for the job (see *Torat Kohanim* and Rashi). This would, of course, parallel the hesitation of Ya'akov and Yosef when they were dressed by Rivka and Pharaoh respectively, as discussed earlier.

be attributed to the different circumstances of the stories, are overshadowed by the unique set of similarities.[68]

At this point, we may ask further, why in the specific case of the priestly robes was there a need for God to intervene and decide on the clothing that would be appropriate for these individuals (thereby also alleviating the normal doubt about the accuracy of the messages transmitted by clothing)? In other words, what about the Temple rite requires God to intervene and show man what he needs to wear? Accordingly, why don't we find such intervention anywhere else in the Torah (besides in the previously mentioned case at the dawn of human history with Adam and Chava)?

Returning to the concept that *tikkun olam* and the model for perfect human communication was demonstrated through the first set of Divine clothes, in the same vein there was a parallel need for perfect *Jewish* communication: Within the *Beit haMikdash*, the Kohanim needed to address the Jewish people in a way that would model such communication. Indeed, it was not just the clothing that was designed by God, it was also the furnishings as well as the structure of the entire compound.

Such an idea is supported by the notion that the Temple represented a microcosm of a perfected world[69] – the experience of *Mikdash* was one of Divine revelation. Had the clothing been designed by man, an admixture of imperfection would have been brought into the experience. Such a mix has its place in the world; indeed, it is the stuff of most of our existence. But in this exceptional place, there was a need for special inspiration about what the world could become if the Jewish people fulfilled their mission of bringing greater awareness of God into the world. We can call such inspiration perfect Jewish communication. In this sanctum of perfection, then, the clothing had to be designed by God in the same way it had been done only once before – at the time of man's thrust into the imperfect world that he would need to fix.

---

68 Indeed, as mentioned in Chapter 1, note 1, there are important parallels between the creation of mankind and the creation of the Jewish people. At the same time, the radically differing circumstances of these two stories would make us expect the parallels to be inexact.

69 See R. Yitzchak Greenburg's monograph entitled "Judaism and Modernity" (Ramat Gan: Lookstein Center, 2006), p. 34.

It bears mentioning that man's original Divine clothing and the clothing of the Kohanim have at least one more thing in common – their *ex post facto* nature. In the original creation, there was no need for clothing. Similarly, before the sin of the golden calf, even though we do find the giving of sacrifices, there is no need for its ritualization through a special building, furnishings and clothing.[70]

Thus, in the ideal world, it would appear that the best type of clothing is none at all, for even Divine clothing is ultimately a *representation* of something else – a perfect representation, but a representation nonetheless. In the case of Tamar, we already pointed out that the Torah tells us that Yehudah *"knows"* her in a situation without clothing. Even as this term is meant to appropriately describe an act of meaningful sexual communion, it is no accident that when it comes to an act that the Torah describes as knowledge, *clothes are nowhere to be found.*

A Postscript – Outer and Inner Modesty

Going back again to where we started, Tamar teaches us more than what clothing cannot be. A deep reading of the same story teaches us what clothing *is* meant to be. When she lived in Yehudah's home as his daughter-in-law, her clothes apparently left little impression. Had they stood out more then, she would have left enough of an impression on Yehudah for him to recognize her later on. Another way of saying this is that her clothing "fit" her so well that they were unnoticed.

Indeed, the opposite of such a scenario is the key to much of the fashion industry – people want to be noticed. Often not remarkable enough without special clothing, the fashion-conscious are looking for an easy (if not always so inexpensive) way to raise their profile. In contrast, clothes that fit our identity are rarely noted. Even flamboyant clothing will not make much of an impression if the person wearing the clothes is already flamboyant without them. In such a case the person will be recognized for who he is and not for what he

---

70 See Seforno on *Shemot* 24:18.

is wearing. His clothing will be a true second skin. What Tamar ultimately teaches us is that anything else ends up being a costume.

The rabbis deduce Tamar's *tzeniut*, her modesty, from the assertion that she covered her face in front of her father-in-law.[71] At the same time, however, this could only be one facet of how she presented herself. Had anything else about her been conspicuous, she would have been more easily recognized by Yehudah. Looking at Tamar more globally, it is likely that the various facets of her personality are interrelated and that her approach as a whole could be broadly described as *tzeniut*. If so, that would mean that *tzeniut* is really much more nuanced and sophisticated than simply covering up one's body.

So how did Tamar relate to clothing in general? We have already seen that she was able to use clothing both to draw attention away from herself (at least according to the rabbis) as well as, when necessary, to draw attention to herself. From this we learn that on a primary social level, clothes can conceal a person's physique and/or they can draw attention to themselves (or, paradoxically, to the body under the clothes). In short, clothing can conceal as well as reveal. Nonetheless, we have also seen that the information revealed by a person's clothes is generally superficial at best and incorrect at worst. That being the case, we would be well advised to wear clothing that draws the least attention to ourselves.[72] (In this regard, bland clothing in places or situations where it is unusual may actually draw more attention than sharper clothing.) In sum, by minimizing attention to our physical appearance, others will be less distracted in their attempt to understand who we really are. This is part of the wisdom of *tzeniut*. But there is more.

Tamar's *tzeniut* teaches us that even revealing our *true* selves should not be a public matter. Hence, when Yehudah did not recognize her "because she covered her face,"[73] it was not only her face that Tamar covered from Yehudah, but her true essence as well. Had Yehudah been more familiar with who Tamar really was, it is unlikely that he would have dismissed her after the death of his older sons in the first place. It would have been even less likely that he would

71 *Sotah* 10b, based on *Bereshit* 38:15.
72 This is really another way of saying what we described before as the moral imperative to wear clothing that honestly represents who we are.
73 *Bereshit* 38:15.

have taken so little interest in her when she was his daughter-in-law that he would not have seen through her disguise later on.

Tamar did not reveal her inner self to Yehudah when she was his daughter-in-law because she must have understood it to be private. If it is to be shared, it is to be shared primarily with God and secondarily with whom one is closest. The inability of a person to really comprehend another without the greatest attention and effort makes it something to encourage only from those with whom we seek an intimate relationship. In this regard, covering our bodies serves as a metaphor for the need to conceal our souls as well.

The Tamar narrative drives home the need to look beyond appearances on the one hand and to keep one's own true essence a private matter on the other. And this is perhaps exactly what the rabbis had in mind when they recognized Tamar as the epitome of true *tzeniut*.[74]

74 *Sotah* 10b.

CHAPTER 7

The Zikaron of Pesach: Productive Selectivity

WHO built the seven gates of Thebes?
The books are filled with names of kings.
Was it the kings who hauled the craggy blocks of stone?
And Babylon, so many times destroyed.
Who built the city up each time? In which of Lima's houses,
That city glittering with gold, lived those who built it?
In the evening when the Chinese wall was finished
Where did the masons go? Imperial Rome
Is full of arcs of triumph. Who reared them up? Over whom
Did the Caesars triumph? Byzantium lives in song.
Were all her dwellings palaces?

(Bertolt Brecht, *A Worker Reads History*)

BRECHT'S MEMORABLE POEM keenly sensitizes us to the subjective nature of any recounting of historical events. This realization explains why it has recently become fashionable to altogether expunge the word "history" from our vocabularies, and to use the word "narrative" in its stead. It is another way of acknowledging that recorded history is necessarily *selective* – otherwise, we would be left with more facts than we can, or would want to, remember. In fact, the study of history can be described as a culture's attempt to discriminate between important events that need to be recorded to better understand itself and less important ones that seem to merely clutter that understanding.

That being the case, the Torah's selective description of events should come as no surprise. Granted, many have correctly pointed out that the Torah does not pretend to be a historical chronicle. At the same time, it cannot be denied that it contains an organized rendering of many historical events in the annals of Jewish history. And, not unlike other historical renderings,[1] it devotes only a few chapters to cover several centuries, while recording other events that transpired in a few days or even minutes in great detail.[2]

Yet, rather than apologizing for this inconsistency as something "unscientific," the Torah presumes that selectivity is a necessary and positive feature. That is to say that it is this very filtering that allows us to make *productive use* of events around us – parallel to the Torah's selectivity, our own minds also assimilate that which is useful and ignore the rest (though like any filter it can also be used for the exact opposite, wherein a person focuses on what is not useful and discards what is – more on this later).

Selectivity not only characterizes the Torah, it is to be seen in the rest of our world's design as well. Just to take one example, our digestive systems break down the food we eat into nutritious and waste elements – much the same as our minds do with events. In both cases, we are provided with items in an "imperfect" form and are given mechanisms through which we can most suitably use them.

Getting Our Attention

It is from such a perspective that the Torah records and pre-separates historical information. But this filtering does not start and end with history. The Torah is equally comfortable with selectivity in what is arguably its main focus – the presentation of its laws. Not all mitzvot are given the same attention. Here too, the Torah shows that some laws require more of our attention, whereas others require less. A particularly apt example of the former is the first time the commandment to observe Pesach through the generations is mentioned.[3]

---

1   Most often, the prehistory of nations is treated in very general fashion before, so to speak, getting to the meat of the story.
2   See Yosef Hayim Yerushalmi's treatment of this in *Zakhor* (New York: Schocken, 1989), pp. 10–13.
3   *Shemot* 12:14–20.

The early command to keep Pesach is anomalous for a variety of reasons. First, all other holidays (as well as further mention of Pesach) are discussed in distinctly legal sections of the Torah. They are to be found in the non-narrative sections that describe the laws of the festivals and give us some accompanying background. By comparison, the initial discussion of Pesach takes place literally in the midst of the Exodus. Moreover, the repeated mention of this holiday as an everlasting statute (*chukat olam*),[4] as well as the generally emphatic tone of this entire section quickly leads us to the conclusion that these laws somehow *needed* greater reinforcement. Finally, and maybe most significantly, we find that the day of Pesach is described as a *zikaron*, a term that is almost always used concerning a physical object.[5]

If in Modern Hebrew *zikaron* has come to mean memory, in Biblical usage it is generally used to describe an object that *elicits* a certain memory. Perhaps it could best be translated as a memory device. So the offering brought by an errant woman (*sotah*) is called a *minchat zikaron*[6] and the tefillin worn between the eyes also described as a *zikaron*.[7] In the first case, the offering is meant to remind her of the immorality of her actions;[8] in the second, the boxes containing verses about the deliverance from Egypt are meant to remind us of that seminal occurrence.

Even beyond its connection to Pesach, however, the notion of *zikaron* is worth explaining. It is clear that there are some objects, especially symbolic items, which evoke memories. Such objects contain a visual or other sensory association to an event, person or object and so easily induce a certain recall. Photographs are only the most vivid and common example of something that we store specifically to stir up a reminiscence. Well aware of the power of memory devices, the Torah recruited objects that it would designate as a

---

4   Ibid., 12:14, 17.
5   The possible exception to this would be the description of Rosh Hashanah as *zi-karon teruah* in *Vayikra* 23:24. There, the term can, nonetheless, also be understood as referring to the *teruah* (the shofar blast) and not to the actual day.
6   *Bemidbar* 5:15.
7   *Shemot* 13:9.
8   Indeed, the rabbis suggest that this highly unusual offering consisting of barley, which in those days was generally animal food, is meant to remind the woman involved to understand that she acted like an animal (*Sotah* 14a).

zikaron specifically in order to create consciousness about certain things at specific times. In this way, then, the Torah is subtly yet effectively mandating the evocation of various salient memories.

Nonetheless, to employ a day as a memory device requires further clarification. As opposed to physical objects, days do not stimulate our senses – without a calendar, we would not easily be able to tell one day from another, since, within any given season, most days are almost completely alike. Moreover, the very idea of commemorating a historical event by marking the day of the year when it happened is not as intuitive as it may sound. In that sense, when Pesach was established, it was a revolutionary concept.

In our own times, the innovative nature of a historical holiday may be hard to fathom, since most contemporary holidays, both secular and religious, commemorate historical events that occurred on the date that they are presently celebrated. This, however, was not always the case. Ancient pagan holidays usually followed the natural cycle of the year, wherein harvests and other natural events were celebrated as they occurred.[9] These holidays were not *commemorations* of past events but palpable celebrations of joyous circumstances in the here and now.

From this perspective, we can understand why the Torah has to emphasize that Pesach is to be a *perpetual* observance. It was to make clear that the Jews were now to celebrate in a highly novel fashion an occurrence that would forever be in their past. It is reasonable that slaves would celebrate on the actual day they are freed (we can make the comparison to a graduation ceremony or other one-time life event). But *commemorating* that day throughout history was not at all obvious to the ancients.

But if the Torah were to truly initiate a revolution in the concept of holidays, it would also need to change how they were observed. For a people to start celebrating a past event would require more than just coloring in that date on the calendar. It would be necessary to create a mechanism by which the day *itself* could become different enough that it could have the same evocative power as a *zikaron*-object. We will now see how the Torah was actually able to do this with Pesach.

---

9   See Abraham Joshua Heschel, *The Sabbath* (New York: The Noonday Press, 1991), p. 7.

Matzah and Memory

It should be noted that the Torah's first discussion of Pesach contains an overwhelming emphasis on the mandate to eat matzah and on the corresponding prohibition to eat or even own *chametz*. Other laws of Pesach of ostensibly equal status, such as eating the Pesach sacrifice or telling over the story (*haggadah*), are not mentioned at all.[10] Moreover, only in this section, which singles out the mandate to eat matzah, is Pesach is referred to as a *zikaron*. By joining these two elements, the Torah appears to be telling us that the unusual Pesach bread serves as the central element transforming this day into a *zikaron* – a memory device.

Furthermore, beyond our previous analysis of the passage in question, the laws of eating matzah stand out in two ways: (1) Generally, when we are commanded in a positive commandment, the inverse does not become prohibited.[11] For example, when we are commanded to don tefillin, we are not prohibited from putting anything else in their place. Likewise, when we are commanded to blow the shofar on Rosh Hashanah, we are not told to refrain from playing any other musical instruments on that day (their prohibition being of later rabbinic origin and having nothing to do specifically with Rosh Hashanah or the shofar). (2) The stringency of violating the inverse (i.e., eating leavened foods) – Divine excision or *karet* – is highly unusual within the context of festival observance. And if this extreme punishment did not make enough of an impression, the Torah repeats the prohibition and its penalty (with slight differences) only a few verses later.

Combined with the emphatic tone of the verses in question, the legal peculiarities just discussed all point to the same thing: the Torah wants us to pay special attention to this commandment. And it wants us to do this on

10   In fact, these two other central commandments are mentioned a few verses later but, whereas the first mention of the holiday is directly from God, the next discussion, where these commandments are given, is via Moshe (*Shemot* 12:21–28).

11   While in many places the Torah gives the same command in both negative and positive versions, here we have two distinct and separate commandments which do not at all need to imply each other. In fact, the observance of Pesach Sheni (see note 15 below) doesn't include the prohibition of *chametz* even though the eating of matzah is commanded (*Pesachim* 9:3).

two levels. First, as previously discussed, the Torah understands that it is commanding the Jews to observe a completely new type of holiday. Since that means that Pesach would be "difficult to sell," it has to emphasize the need to keep the holiday altogether.[12] But this alone doesn't explain why the Torah singles out the eating of matzah from the other commandments of Pesach. Thus, secondly – and perhaps even more important – by putting such a strong stress on matzah, the Torah is saying that it is specifically this practice that will somehow carve the festival into the Jewish psyche. But why is that?

As with commemorative holidays in general, our familiarity with holiday foods can blur the revolutionary nature of marshalling their multi-sensual experience to remind us of certain events and accordingly give tangible content to a date. In fact, it was quite conventional to hold banquets in celebration of pagan holidays. The Torah's addition was that the Pesach banquet would center on symbolic foods which would specifically be associated with historical memories. In the present case, the simple, hastily baked bread conveys both the hurriedness of the Exodus and the poverty of the slavery in Egypt. Moreover, since the Torah puts such a strong stress on this mitzvah, we are more likely to look carefully at the details of its particular ritual object in order to allow it to effectively evoke the desired frame of mind.

The Torah understood that without matzah or something like it, celebrating Pesach would run the risk of artifice, commemorating an event without triggering an actual memory of that event or its meaning. Indeed, this is the problem of many contemporary holidays where the commemoration and the event we are commemorating rarely fit together organically. Hence, we usually have to strain to identify what turkeys really have to do with Thanksgiving or barbequed meat with Yom Ha'atzma'aut. For a commemoration to have straightforward meaning, it must recreate an *experience*. But not any type of

---

12 It is intuitive that the less likely we believe someone will heed a command, the greater our need to emphasize it and provide ample reward and/or punishment to reinforce its fulfillment. Such an idea finds further substantiation in the mitzvah of the sabbatical year, obviously a difficult one to impose on a heavily agrarian society. There we find a highly unusual emphasis of the commandment's reward, certainly meant to engender greater observance of a mitzvah that, true to the Torah's expectation, had a historically mixed performance record.

experience – the experience has to be personal and not simply something that happened to other people. For this reason the rabbis famously proclaim that the Pesach tale cannot be told without the presence of matzah,[13] thereby turning it into a personal memory which, like all personal memories, can be relived.

Going back to our discussion of memory devices, based on what we have considered thus far, the Torah could have easily described matzah as the *zikaron* of Pesach – as the device that could logically evoke the main themes of the holiday. But for all of its centrality, matzah remains only one piece of the composition that the Torah creates here.

In fact, Pesach contains other important memory-evoking elements. The bitter herbs are an obvious reminder of the bitterness of slavery, and the *haggadah* potently fills our imaginations with the events of the story. Within this scheme, matzah serves as the vanguard of a multifaceted effort to saturate the Jew with the memories that transport him back to the historical Exodus that he is celebrating. Through the combination of these memories it is the *day itself* that goes from being a commemoration of a historical event to the celebration of a current one.

In sum, various individual memory devices coalesce to make the *day* of Pesach tangibly different from the days before and after it. In being made into a *zikaron*, Pesach is crafted to the point where it becomes something perceivable to our very senses. As a result, what starts with matzah ends up being so much more.

Of course, one could still ask why Pesach is the only holiday that the Torah calls a *zikaron*. One would think that the Torah would follow the strategy explained above for all of the holidays in order to maximize their effectiveness. Yet the reason it doesn't lies in the difference between the creation of a new paradigm and subsequent items modeled in its wake. Since Pesach is the first historical commemoration experienced by the Jewish people, it creates the paradigm. Once the concept of a *zikaron*-holiday was established by Pesach, there was no need for the other holidays to re-establish it. Hence, the other historical holiday(s) of the Torah,[14] most notably Sukkot, don't need to be

13   *Mechilta, Shemot* 13:8.
14   It is true that even Pesach and Sukkot have a seasonal agricultural theme and that

mentioned in the middle of the historical narratives that they commemorate. Neither is there a need to insist on their perpetual observance, to reinforce their central rituals or to create a cluster of mitzvot to enhance their identity. Once the ice is broken with Pesach, Sukkot for example can simply follow the idea already created.[15] Hence, it can suffice with a single experiential, memory-evoking obligation – to live in huts so as to remember the desert experience.[16] Since we now understand the notion of a historical commemoration, the Torah does not need a *force-majeure* to activate that understanding.

Beyond our explanation, however, it is worthwhile mentioning the tremendous emphasis the Torah generally places on remembering the Exodus from Egypt.[17] In this context, Pesach appears to be too central to the theology and mission of the Jewish people for the Torah to be satisfied with our latent attention. Since there is no parallel emphasis on remembering the desert experience commemorated by Sukkot, the proper internalization of that experience is of *comparatively* less consequence.

Whatever the reason for the Torah's special treatment of Pesach, the unrivaled number of Jews who observe the holiday and have an idea of what it is about indicates the success of the Torah's *zikaron* strategy. The memory device has worked.

◆ ◆ ◆

Like the Jews who left Egypt, there are many events in our lives which form our personalities. But then we also experience many other events that do not

---

the other holidays have also become associated with historical events. Nonetheless, Pesach and Sukkot stand out in their explicit connection to specific occurrences.

15 This idea is further supported by the unusual institution of Pesach Sheni, which allows those who are not able to celebrate Pesach, to celebrate an abbreviated version of the holiday one month later (*Bemidbar* 9:9–12). This is clearly not the case with the Torah's other holidays.

16 The Torah command to wave the *lulav* on the first day of Sukkot seems to have little to do with any historical consciousness of the day (see *Sukkah* 37b-38a). In any case, even if we include this commandment, the observance of Sukkot mandated by the Torah still remains more rudimentary than Pesach.

17 Ramban on *Shemot* 13:16 brings this most eloquently to our attention, while at the same time giving many examples of other commandments designed to remind us of the Exodus.

make us who we are. The difference between the former and the latter is, to a large extent, a matter of choice. Likewise, the Torah *chose* to greatly highlight the Exodus from Egypt and make it arguably the seminal event in Jewish history. When it comes to our personal life narratives, however, it is mostly up to us to determine what we will emphasize as its highlights. Unfortunately, most of us are not even sufficiently self-aware to realize how much power over our own experiences this gives us. The good news is that it can still be otherwise.

I am not suggesting that we focus only on the "good" in order to attain some sort of vacuous bliss. Rather, we need to emulate the Torah's mode of selectivity, sometimes focusing on positive memories, other times on negative ones, in order to develop to our maximum potential.

In this vein, Rav Shlomo Wolbe *z"l* follows the Slobodka school of mussar, telling us that we must develop our own sense of greatness before we engage in self-criticism.[18] In truth, both steps are critical. First the realization of what we can offer, based on an optimistic evaluation of ourselves, followed by a highly critical analysis of where we have fallen short of our potential. In this type of a project, being overly objective will actually be counterproductive. For the resultant alternative of taking a neutral overview of our aggregate performance can too easily lead to an "I'm ok, you're ok"–style mediocrity.

But there is more. Selectivity is not only useful in developing our personal potential, it is equally important for interacting with others and with the community. Whether we are aware of it or not, our mere participation in a community automatically requires us to see things in a way that, at least partially, reflects its collective vision. Moreover, accepting communal visions that are necessarily different from our own personal ones provides a good stepping stone to recognizing the legitimacy of the visions of other individuals and communities as well. Once we take one step out of our own thinking, it is much easier to take the second and third. Hence, the process that starts with appreciating the selectivity of our visions is what allows us to make room for the multiple legitimate visions within our community and ultimately outside of it as well.

18　See, for example, *Alei Shor*, vol. 1 (Be'er Ya'akov, Israel: Otzar haSefarim, 1978), pp. 8–70.

As mentioned, the Torah doesn't stop at the legitimacy of selectivity. It insists on using that selectivity with wisdom. To admit the selectivity of our narratives can all too easily allow us to become morally tepid relativists. Far from such a situation, the Torah indicates that we are expected to consider the implications of how we choose to view things. Though selectivity is a part of everyone's life, *productive* selectivity is a way to emulate God.

AFTERWORD

IN MY PREVIOUS book, I wrote about the important role of new interpretation toward making the Torah the book of contemporary value and interest that it was meant to be. At the beginning of the present volume, we spoke about another reason we must continue to interpret and reinterpret the Torah. We spoke about the individualized conversation with God that can be had in dynamic interpretive Torah study. In fact, what is available is more than conversation.

Interpretation is really another word for discovery, a distinctively powerful human experience. Through this process, we take an object outside of ourselves and figure out its place in our own personal world. And when we do so, we acquire something in a much more fundamental way than anything we can purchase.

For better or worse, however, most interpretation occurs near the time of our first encounter with an object. Once we have given it its personal meaning, it is rare for us to want to reexamine it. Each time we reencounter the item in question and it fits our original interpretation, we become more certain about the correctness of our understanding. It is only in rare cases that, after encountering a great deal of evidence that contradicts our original interpretation and, usually kicking and screaming, we agree to reevaluate our original interpretation. All this in itself is not so bad. The real problem is that our general satisfaction with our initial understanding eventually makes us numb, to the point where there is no longer any need for interpretation whatsoever.

When the rabbis say that the Torah wants us to read its words as if they were constantly new,[1] it means that we need to interpret them each and every time we learn them. Granted, we may come up with the same interpretation as we did the last time, but we still have to engage in the act of interpretation each time we encounter a Torah text and not simply look at it with the intuitive comfort that we understand it already.

By asking us to constantly interpret the Torah, we are being asked to constantly personalize it. More than anything else, it is this constant search that gives life to the Jewish people's relationship with the Torah's Author.

In this context, the rabbinic statement that the Torah has seventy faces is both puzzling and revealing. Postmodernist thinkers might endorse this thought and add that really everything has seventy faces; that interpretation is necessarily personal and consequently anything we interpret is intrinsically multifaceted. In that case, what justification is there in singling out the Torah for such treatment?

While we can and should have a relationship with everything that we encounter, most things that we come across are not deserving of a great deal of attention. The same cannot be said about Torah – the relationship of man to Torah and, via it, to its Author, is paramount to our existence. As such, it is the one thing whose multiple interpretations we must seek each time we encounter it. We must do this for the knowledge thereby revealed, but even more so for the living relationship thereby created. If the essays in this book have succeeded in allowing some readers to rediscover certain sections of the Torah and thus to reengage in relationship with its Author, I will consider myself very fortunate.

---

1   *Sifrei* on *Devarim* 6:6.

ABOUT THE AUTHOR

RABBI FRANCIS NATAF is the Educational Director of the David Cardozo Academy in Jerusalem and the author of *Redeeming Relevance in the Book of Genesis* (Urim: 2006). He has also published numerous articles concerning Jewish education, Bible and Jewish thought. Rabbi Nataf was ordained at Yeshiva University and holds degrees in Jewish history and international affairs.

ABOUT THE ARTIST

BARBARA LADIN FISHER is a Judaic artist who has been commissioned to design and make over sixty Torah Mantles. Her Judaic works are located in synagogues and homes in the United States, Canada and Israel. Barbara lives in Atlanta, Georgia, with her husband Mark, and they are the parents of five. You can view her other works at www.bfisherjudaica.com or contact her at barblfisher@yahoo.com.

Publication of this book was assisted by
The David Cardozo Academy
Machon Ohr Aaron & Betsy Spijer
7 Cassuto St.
Jerusalem 96433 Israel.
cacademy@012.net.il
www.cardozoschool.org